Off the Wall

Zeina Maasri

OFFthe
WALL

Political Posters of the
Lebanese Civil War

I.B. TAURIS

LONDON · NEW YORK

First published in 2009 by I.B.Tauris & Co. Ltd
London • New York
Reprinted 2009, 2016
www.ibtauris.com

ISBN: 978 1 84511 951 5

A full CIP record for this book is available from
the British Library
A full CIP record is available from the Library
of Congress

Library of Congress Catalog Card Number: available

This publication was made possible with the partial
support of the Lebanese Association for Plastic
Arts, Ashkal Alwan, through a grant provided by
the Foundation Open Society Institute.

This book is in conjunction with the ongoing
project and exhibition *Signs of Conflict: Political Posters
of Lebanon's Civil War* by Zeina Maasri. The exhibition
was produced by the Lebanese Association for
Plastic Arts, Ashkal Alwan, with the support of the
Heinrich Böll Foundation in the framework of Home
Works IV: A Forum on Cultural Practices, Beirut,
12 April–1 May 2008.

Page design by Zeina Maasri
Typeset in Fedra Sans and Fedra Serif B
Printed and bound in Great Britain by Page Bros

To Amin and Samira

CONTENTS

POSTERS

Chapter 2: Leadership

1978. Anonymous. 60 × 44 cm

2.2 *1 May, Jumblatt's international day.* Lebanese National Movement, 1977. Oussama. 69 × 50 cm

2.3 *16 March 1978, the first annual commemoration of the martyr leader Kamal Jumblatt.* Lebanese National Movement, 1978. Anonymous. 70 × 50 cm

2.4 *Offering life gave a new understanding to the liberation struggle – Kamal Jumblatt.* Lebanese National Movement, 1979. Hassib al-Jassem. 61 × 44 cm

2.5 *Together until victory.* Lebanese National Movement, 1978. Aref el-Rayess. 71 × 50 cm

2.6 *16 March.* Progressive Socialist Party, c.1985. Ghazi Saab. 70 × 50 cm

2.7 *The 10th commemoration of the martyrdom of Kamal Jumblatt, 1917–1977.* Progressive Socialist Party, 1987. Imad Abou Ajram. 61 × 43 cm

2.8 *Jumblatt did not die, you who call for submissive solutions.* Lebanese National Movement, 1977. Anonymous. 50 × 70 cm

2.9 *Just like Abd-el-Nasser, Jumblatt will remain the symbol of an Arab revolution.* Lebanese National Movement, 1977. Anonymous. 50 × 70 cm

2.10 *Jumblatt gave his life for the Palestinian cause and a united Arab destiny.* Lebanese National Movement, 1978. Anonymous. 50 × 70 cm

2.11 *The Lebanon of Kamal Jumblatt is a fortress of Arab steadfastness.* Lebanese National Movement, 1978. Anonymous. 50 × 70 cm

2.12 *16 March 1985. Pledge and loyalty.* Progressive Socialist Party, 1985. Mahmoud Zeineddine. 60 × 47 cm

2.13 *A pledge is a pledge.* Progressive Socialist Party, 1981. Nabil Kdouh. 65 × 50 cm

2.14 *Over time our weapons are the guarantee.* Progressive Socialist Party, 1984. Anonymous

2.15 *Our Lebanon needs you, YOU.* Lebanese Forces, c.1983. Pierre Sadek. 66 × 48 cm

2.16 Portrait of Bashir Gemayel when elected president. Lebanese Kataeb, 1982. Varoujan. 95 × 64 cm

2.17 *23 August.* Lebanese Forces, 1983. Pierre Sadek. 66 × 44 cm

2.18 *14 September.* Lebanese Forces, 1983. Raidy. 66 × 47 cm

2.19 Portrait of Mussa al-Sadr. Amal movement, 1978. Anonymous. 69 × 49 cm

2.20 *Holder of trust from the bearer of trust.* Amal movement, c.1980. Anonymous. 42 × 60 cm

2.21 *Israel is an absolute evil.* Hizbullah, 1985. Muhammad Ismail. 60 × 22 cm

2.22 *Al-Sayyed Mussa al-Sadr was like a son to me – Khomeini. We have to form a culture of war and employ all resources in our battle with Israel – Mussa al-Sadr.* Hizbullah, c.1985. Anonymous. 64 × 42 cm

Chapter 3: Commemoration

Chapter 5: Belonging

FOREWORD

Posters as Weapons

Fawwaz Traboulsi

Question: Why should we remember a civil war? Answer: so as not to have it repeated. A more difficult one: what should be remembered of a civil war? Certainly not all things can be remembered. But many things should, mainly causes and lessons. But many other things should be forgotten. Yes, forgotten. As you can only forget what you know. Hence, back to memory. Forgetting is one thing, amnesia is another.

Amnesia, both officialized and popular, has been rampant in post-war Lebanon. Collective amnesia, like individual amnesia, is a form of repression of memory that involves a number of complex mechanisms. It resorts to breaking up links between memorable events and to ways of substitution, condensation and displacement quite similar to those that operate in dreams. The Lebanese wars (1975–90) are represented in the hegemonic and amnesic discourse as the 'war of others' or, in a more diluted form, the war 'for the others'. By this process, amnesia condenses multiple causality into one single cause, transfers guilt and blocks the narration of memory and reflection. Fifteen years are reduced to one denomination, *al-Harb al-Lubnaniya*: 'the Lebanese war', strangely enough named 'Lebanese' whilst its causes and protagonists are deemed all external or externalized. More, the long years of fighting, bloodshed, displacement and suffering soon come to be encapsulated into what resembles a natural catastrophe, say an earthquake. Post-war reconstruction is thus represented as the 'reconstruction' of an international trade centre in downtown Beirut, symbol of a magical revival of a glorious age of economic prosperity and communal coexistence. Amnesia again *delinks* causes and effects and blocks the obvious spontaneous question: if the pre-war period was a 'golden age', why did it produce such a horrible war? The tautological answer comes back: no relation; it was a 'war of the others'.

How did the 'others' succeed in getting the Lebanese to wage 'their wars' with such enthusiasm and kill so many among themselves 'for them'? And the vicious circle goes on and on.

For those reasons, and for others, collective amnesia is pathological while it pretends to be curative. Contrary to its pretence of relieving the patient of bloody memories and traumatic events, it does the opposite: it condemns the patient to live and re-enact that traumatic *past* as a permanent *present*. That is why the post-war years have been lived as a 'cold civil war' awaiting the 'return' of the hotter version.

Zeina Maasri's remarkable achievement in this first work of hers is to draw the dividing lines between amnesia and memory. With patience, perseverance and a lot of talent she has managed to collect, document and archive hundreds of posters produced by the different protagonists during the wars of Lebanon. What makes this remarkable contribution to collective memory more valuable is that it has been undertaken by a single courageous individual, at a time when institutions and NGOs have shrunk from it.

But Zeina Maasri has done much more than that. She has analysed the posters in content and form, critically adapting a number of theoretical tools for that purpose.

To begin with, the posters were contextualized, and partially historicized, as historicizing remains the sure antidote to amnesia. Maasri does not fall into the trap that content analysts often fall into by assuming that there should always be a 'hegemonic' discourse to be sought for. She analyses a multiplicity of discourses that mutate and morph from their early modernist pretences into their later openly sectarian and identitarian selves.

The author is also careful to differentiate between civil war posters and propaganda posters. Despite the fact that the former contain elements of propaganda, their messages tend to be less concerned with subverting and demoralizing the 'enemy' than with boosting collective narcissism and mobilizing for additional reasons to die. After all, you rarely defect in a civil war. You might desert. But you would not expect 'enemy' fighters to defect, inasmuch as you would not yourself defect, as your fates in both cases will be death. The logic of the tribe has it that 'blood never turns into water'.

Posters say a lot about the war.

In this book, the war talks with pictures and words lauding disappeared leaders, and awaiting their return, and militias compete in claiming disputed territories, or a whole homeland. And as much as each protagonist's 'homeland' shrinks, in that same proportion, its own tribal-religious space is further socialized, as a delirium of violence and identity explodes.

The poster is contextualized once more to provide a background for the development of the art of the Arab poster, and specifically in the shared Lebanese–Palestinian experience, detailing producers and funders, artists, and the varieties of experiences in poster creation.

Finally, Zeina did not fail to notice the deterioration of the artistic and aesthetic quality of the poster as the tribalized religious sects shed their modernist garb and wear the militarized uniforms of murderous identities.

Civil wars are the ideal domain of the symbolic. Prolonged and inconclusive civil wars come to inflate their symbolic charge as battles are frustratingly incapable of ascent to the ultimate terminal stage that determines victory for the one, defeat for the others. The conflict then involves an additional dose of symbolic duels in which violence increases its extra-military functions. Such duels aim at inflicting as many symbolic wounds on the 'other' as possible. The protagonists of the Lebanese civil wars invented many ways of inflicting such wounds: verbal duels of swear words and vilification across the dividing lines (transmitted by loudspeakers, walkie-talkies or phones); offensive graffiti on walls; desacralization of sacred sites; abduction; humiliating treatment at checkpoints; not to speak of rape, which seems to have a dubiously limited occurrence in the Lebanese wars. The last three forms of violence are called symbolic in the sense that the physical harm done to the individual is intended as a symbolic harm to the whole community.

Here, the symbolic is never disassociated from action. The symbolic charges action with added impetus. Now, the 'individuation of the enemy' directs the sniper's hunt in which 'killing any one of them' is the equivalent of 'killing them all'; and the sacralized territory demands, at times by the intersection of holy men and women, to be desacralized by purging with blood and fire those who have soiled it. The Lebanese wars were pioneers in ethnic cleansing.

Posters, so well defined by Maasri as symbolic sites of the political struggle, soon become symbolic sites of the military struggle.

The German art historian Horst Bredekamp evokes the 'aliveness' of images, in his theory of the picture act, *Bildakt*.[1] He posits that pictures do not merely illustrate, they emerge in ever new forms of 'vivification' and by so doing acquire a 'reflexive' role. I do not know to what extent Bredekamp's theory can be applied to all visual representations. But one thing seems very likely: the picture act theory fits well into the relationship between art and war, between images and violence, when images can become substitutes for real action or real achievements.

No wonder that Bredekamp illustrates his theory with examples of violence that pictures provoke. He reminds us, for example, of a famous photo of an insurgent aiming a lance at a photo of Ceauşescu. Since the insurgent could not directly take hold of the visage of the Romanian dictator, he directed his punitive action at the picture. More recently, news agencies wired a photo of Egyptian demonstrators trampling down a big picture of president Hosni Mubarak during the 6 May 2008 general strike of protest against the rising cost of living.

Every day, posters are torn in the streets of the cities of the world at the hands of persons who object to their messages. But you might not be content with wounding a poster with a knife or lance; you might attempt to kill a poster.

Deranged men have often attacked works of art, knifed a canvas or disfigured a mural or a sculpture for reasons that remain largely personal, psychic. But those individual acts are the exception that proves the collective rule. The Romanian insurgent and the Cairo demonstrators are not committing a collective act, they look very much like people engaged in political assassination.

Pictures and images in the large sense of the word can be so dangerous they need to be protected by bodyguards and bulletproof material against violence. Picasso's *Guernica* is a case in point. It is still displayed behind a thick glass cage in the annexe of the Prado Museum in Madrid, half a century after the event that drove the artist to its creation. Next to it stands on vigil an armed member of the Guardia Civil. Picasso's mural in its home town is being protected from a different threat. In fact, it is being protected from a *deranged* someone acting in the name of a group suffering from 'wounds of memory' left unhealed since the 1936–9 Spanish Civil War!

As I am writing these words, a Palestinian friend sent me photos he shot as he was travelling in the Nablus area, of posters still hanging in the centre of the village of 'Aqraba showing the contradictory resilience of Saddam Hussein's memory among Palestinians. In the three of them, the dictator is shown in military attire: in one, he is dressed in military fatigues, and in the other two, shooting away with a Kalashnikov automatic rifle. Under one of the posters, Saddam is depicted as 'Master of all martyrs, leader, mujahid, and martyr: Saddam, the Glorious'. It could be inferred from the photos that they were hung by the municipality or by some influential notable. But this did not deter Palestinians who had a different idea of the Iraqi dictator from riddling two of the posters with bullet holes.

The same could be said about the famous Iraqi tankist who, retreating from Kuwait in March 1991, directed his tank's cannon to shatter a wall posting Saddam Hussein's portrait in the southern city of Basra. This symbolic act sparked an intifada of tens of thousands of southern Iraqis against the Baghdad regime. Clearly, that tankist could not foresee the effect of his act. He was merely reacting violently to the challenge of the mere visual presence a man he considers responsible for so much bloody repression and humiliation of his people.

Wars say a lot about posters.

If posters did not exude such a big dose of challenge, why would they provoke such violent reactions?

In her reading of war through posters and of posters in the light of wars, Zeina Maasri has offered us another way of looking at posters: posters as weapons.

PREFACE

Much has been written on Lebanon's civil war, with varying perspectives on the conflict and through different forms of writing – historical accounts, social and economic studies, personal narratives and biographies. However, little attention if any has been paid to the visual culture that resulted from this war. With the exception of Maria Chakhtoura's book *La guerre des graffiti*, which surveys street graffiti in Beirut between 1975 and 1977, no other publication has addressed the interrelation of visual production and political struggle during the civil war in Lebanon.

The idea for this book started in 2003 as I came across the collection of political posters dating from the 1960s to the 1980s available in the Libraries Special Collections and Archive at the American University of Beirut. After looking through the collection I began my research with the premise that narratives of Lebanon's wartime conflicts, far from being restricted to texts, are carried through the political posters issued within that period. I was interested in studying how the political discourses of the different Lebanese warring factions were visually materialized and diffused through the poster format. I also began locating and interviewing authors of posters, in an attempt to understand a number of issues, including their motivations in designing political posters, the conditions of their practice and aesthetic underpinnings to their work. As my research progressed, I needed to make sense of the role these posters held within the context of Lebanon's civil war. I became dissatisfied with the concept of the propaganda poster, which has been the subject of numerous studies on cases of state warfare and post-revolution nation-building – the First and Second World Wars, Soviet Russia, Cuba, China and Iran. These cases and the subsequent conception of political posters as an all-encompassing unified state

propaganda do not apply to Lebanon's wartime posters. I realized that a conceptualization of political posters in the context of civil war was to be done in this book.

A major aspect of the research I have undertaken in the past years lies in the collection, documentation and digital archiving of these posters. The collection available
in the AUB libraries, although significant, does not cover either a complete spectrum
of the different warring factions or the full length of the war. I thus embarked on
a laborious task of collecting posters from different sources: party archives, library
collections outside Lebanon, private collections and partisans. It's through this process that I encountered the difficulty of accessing such material and a local neglect of
posters, deemed ephemeral artefacts not worthy of preservation.

The war brought massive destruction. A number of places in which personal or
institutional archives were kept did not elude the damage caused by 15 years of civil
strife and recurrent invasions. Add to that Israel's war on Lebanon in the summer of
2006; I had just finished documenting around a hundred posters of the Hizbullah collection and a few months later no trace was left of the building housing the posters.
Many political parties reported that their archive, if it did not suffer direct damage
during the civil war, got stolen, or purposely sabotaged and vandalized. Moreover,
partisans who held their own collections of posters have had to destroy these among
other evidence that linked them to a political faction. This has happened recurrently
in the aftermath of territorial gains of one camp over another and mostly in consequence of repeated invasions by foreign armies, which forced political activities of
certain parties to go underground.

Nevertheless, I managed to document into a digital database around five hundred posters, in addition to what was already available from the AUB library archive.
The database enables easy access and customized search through the posters, which
has been instrumental for the purpose of analysis, whence my study in this book. My
intention is to render this database accessible through an online archive that could
provide insightful research material for other interested scholars and students. The
posters unfold the narratives of the prevailing political conflicts as much as they
provide insight into the history of modern Arab visual culture and local graphic design practice. The database has already been successfully put into use in contemporary artistic productions and by my students in a seminar course I taught at the
American University of Beirut. Through my fieldwork for this research, poster collection and encounters with authors, I came across significant material that did not
find its place in this book. This will be the subject of my ongoing study on political
posters and future collaborative projects centred on the history of the Arab poster as
a modern creative practice intrinsic to the cultural production of a given time and

place. Meanwhile, I hope that this book and the online poster archive will contribute to and promote further scholarship on this stimulating yet unattended-to local cultural artefact.

Zeina Maasri

ACKNOWLEDGEMENTS

I am first and foremost grateful to the individuals, archive institutions and the few political parties that have kept a poster collection and generously shared it with me for the purpose of this study. I would like to specially acknowledge the poster collection that has been preserved over the years at the American University of Beirut Library and the efforts done by the Digital Documentation Centre to render this collection public on the university website. Without their initial endeavour, I wouldn't have thought to embark on this present work. I am greatly thankful to the individuals who shared their poster collections and personal archives with me: Armand Bachaalani, Karl Bassil, Abbudi Bou Jawde, Wassim Jabre, Randa Shaath and Adnan Sharara. I am particularly indebted to the artist and collector Adnan Sharara, who has entrusted me with his formidable poster collection, and to Abbudi Bou Jawde for his continuous support on this project and his resolute efforts to jointly establish an archive centre for Arab posters.

I would like to express my thanks to the political parties that have been cooperative in granting me access to their poster archives and sharing valuable information on the party media activities during the war. I want to individually thank the artists who shared their experiences with me and contributed valuable insights on political posters: Charbel Fares, Waddah Fares, Kameel Hawa, Hawarian, Muhammad Ismail, Nabil Kdouh, Tammouz Knayzeh, Mounir Maasri, Emil Menhem, Muhammad Moussalli, Ghazi Saab, Pierre Sadek and Helmi el-Touni.

I am greatly thankful to the Lebanese Association for Plastic Arts, Ashkal Alwan, which provided a contribution for publishing this book and produced the related exhibition *Signs of Conflict* in the framework of Home Works IV: A Forum on

Cultural Practices. Christine Tohme of Ashkal Alwan has been a keen supporter of this project, and I am grateful for her help. I also gratefully acknowledge the grant awarded by the American University of Beirut for this project. It has greatly aided my research in many ways, including the documentation of posters. I am grateful to Abigail Fielding-Smith and Jayne Hill of I.B.Tauris for bringing this publication to fruition and to Merlin Cox for his meticulous copy-editing of the manuscript.

    This book has been many years in the making and would not have been possible without the support and encouragement of friends and colleagues. I wish to thank them here, Howayda Al-Harithy who is always ready to offer valuable advice on my research and for reading and commenting on the manuscript; Fawwaz Traboulsi for his encouraging feedback on the manuscript and for writing a wonderful foreword to the book; Marwan Ghandour for his diligent reading and meticulous editing of the introduction; Rania Ghosn, Josette Khalil and Alia Karame, who provided precious input and assisted me in many tasks at different stages of the project; my students at AUB who listened to this material as I gave it in a seminar course and responded with a lot of enthusiasm and stimulating debates; Saleh Barakat, Samir Frangié, Samir Sayegh and Kirsten Scheid who generously shared resourceful information on the subject of this study; Raja Abillama, Pierre Abi Saab, Samer Frangié, Khaled Malas, Dagmar Reichert and Jana Traboulsi for their kind support and friendly advice throughout the whole process; and finally, Joseph Samaha, to whom I owe my interest in politics.

    This book is dedicated to my father, for the long sessions of fiery political discussion, and to the wonderful women in my family, Samira, Jaqueline and Affaf, whose resilience and generosity in life have greatly marked me.

PART I

The Poster in Context

INTRODUCTION

Political Posters
as Symbolic Sites of Struggle

During the 15 years of civil war (1975–90), political posters filled the streets and charged the walls of cities all over Lebanon. As the ongoing war formed an intrinsic aspect of everyday life in Lebanon, the graphic signs and political rhetoric of posters became a prevalent sight/reading that shaped the cityscape. The political parties strove to legitimize and sustain their political struggle while battling for power and territorial control. Their military engagement on the battlefronts was coupled with a relentless battle of signs and symbolic appropriation of territory through extensive poster production and distribution.

Lebanon's civil war is a complex case where local socio-economic and sectarian struggles, linked with regional politics, characterized political discourses and distinguished the numerous warring factions. That, in turn, materialized in the production of an equally complex plethora of political posters, with diverse iconography and conflicting significations, as well as distinct aesthetic practices. There were at least twenty ideologically distinct Lebanese political factions. These factions managed to gather around them a substantial number of partisans and fighters, ready to assume the severe consequences of their political acts.

How to make sense of political posters' nature of operation in the context of civil war? How does one political poster, out of many on the same wall, hail to a specific person and at once be contested by another? And how do we account for the substantial number of citizens who refused to take part in the fighting, adhered to none of the factions, yet sympathized with the political discourse of a certain poster and felt threatened by another?

Beyond the polarity of propaganda/activism

Popular speech, as well as academic studies, refers to political posters as a form of 'propaganda', often in the derogatory sense of the term, denouncing the persuasive and manipulative functions that are embedded in deceitful messages. Conversely, political posters of a civil protest type usually elude the 'propaganda' label and are considered a form of activism, commended for their political participation and commitment to a just cause. Between these two attitudes, there are attempts at appreciating or at least examining the aesthetics of the political posters despite their 'propaganda' content. With these efforts, titles such as 'the art of propaganda', 'the art of persuasion' and 'the art of the political poster' emerge, whereby the 'art' qualifier subsumes the political into artistic practices, hence deserving review. Neither these reconciliatory titles nor the polarity between propaganda and activism adequately explain the polemical nature of political posters. Who decides which posters are propaganda and which are activist? What are the criteria? Is it the type of message, or the institution that lies behind the poster production, or both?

David Crowley in a chapter entitled 'The Propaganda Poster' distinguishes between different forms of political posters: a celebratory one produced by professionals and state officials and an agitational one produced by amateurs with little resources.[1] Crowley notes that the critique raised in England of the propaganda methods used by the state during the First World War, in addition to the investment in propaganda by totalitarian regimes, mounted public concern and 'accentuated the sense of fear attached to the concept'.[2] He observes that during the Cold War, Western democratic states refrained from the creation of 'explicit graphic propaganda', since these states considered an 'espousal of free speech and the right of all peoples to self-determination did not sit comfortably with overt campaigns to mould public opinion'.[3]

What Crowley does not address is that these same democratic states resorted to other forms of mass media through which new methods of 'propaganda' were developed. These new methods were probably not as 'explicit' but not less 'moulding', as is argued by Noam Chomsky in *Media Control: The Spectacular Achievements of Propaganda*. Chomsky writes that these new forms of mass media are developed 'not like a totalitarian state, where it's done by force. These achievements [the spectacular achievements of propaganda] are under conditions of freedom'.[4] While Western states turned to other means of political propaganda, Crowley argues that the political poster in the 1960s became a tool of protest and counter-culture activism:

> With a few exceptions, in the West the state's interest in the propaganda poster began to decline in the 1950s. . . . It seemed in the West that the prospect of the kinds of political

agitation experienced between the wars was increasingly remote. Yet these certainties were shaken by a new wave of strong-willed activism. . . . The late 1950s saw the emergence of new kinds of politics concerned with moral and ethical issues, and the extension of civil rights . . . New issues became the focus of Left-wing dissent; civil rights for ethnic minorities and women; atomic weapons; and, from the mid-1960s, the war in Vietnam. . . . Such direct approaches to political activism were extolled in the late 1960s by sections of the counter-culture who sought to politicize all aspects of everyday life: 'The personal,' it was pronounced, 'is the political'.[5]

In her acclaimed book *Graphic Agitation: Social and Political Graphics Since the Sixties* Liz McQuiston distinguishes in the cases of national politics between the official voice, 'the establishment', which includes 'governments, leaders, and institutions that operate systems of control and define societal values and priorities', and the unofficial voice, which 'belongs to those who question, criticize or even reject those systems and structures as well as the motives of people behind them'. She considers that both voices rely on propaganda techniques, even if they have widely different access to resources. McQuiston considers propaganda to be 'part of the official voice that aims to win votes and to set policies; but is also part of the unofficial voice that protests against the established order or encourages dissent'.[6] She acknowledges that both the establishment and the anti-establishment resort to propaganda techniques, whether to win consent or to rouse dissent. However, when she discusses conditions outside US national politics, the polarity between propaganda and activism reappears, where she associates propaganda and manipulation of public opinion with centralized powers exercised by 'one ideological voice' and 'repressive regimes'. Furthermore, she does not use the term 'propaganda' when discussing protest and activist graphics pertaining to issues of liberation, pro-democracy, anti-war, social change and youth politics, among other grass-roots and popular resistance movements.

I fully appreciate the framework within which McQuiston examines activist graphics as 'examples of graphic design as a force for social development and change' but I remain sceptical of the bipolar distinction between propaganda and activism. This polarity removes possibilities of envisioning propaganda strategies in activist quests and, conversely, disregards emancipatory motives in propaganda. Methods of propaganda vary with the complex forms in which power is articulated and perceived, the ways political discourses are constructed, whether through hegemonic or counter-hegemonic means.

The problem here is the unresolved definition of 'propaganda' in poster design and how it operates in the public domain. The term is referred to as a means to publicize political positions regardless of institution and message, and is used elsewhere as an attribute to denounce 'manipulative' and repressive political rhetoric. A quick look at debates occurring on web forums concerned with political posters or comments on related articles immediately reveals the fragility of such a categorization. The Cuban OSPAAAL (Organization of Solidarity with the People of Africa, Asia and Latin America) posters are but one example out of many political posters that reveal how simplistic the propaganda/activism distinction is. For what qualifies within a liberal mind frame as posters of solidarity with third-world liberation and other subaltern struggles is dismissed by right-wing Americans for instance as Communist propaganda. Another example is the posters in support of the Palestinian cause, particularly of the late 1960s and 70s, which are often easily denounced as mere tools of propaganda though they were produced not by a clearly established state but by various organizations and independent individuals.

The polarity between propaganda and activism fails to apply, as a model of analysis, to political posters during Lebanon's civil war. We are obviously not confronted with an all-encompassing hegemonic state propaganda since a consensual state endeavour collapsed in the face of antagonistic political factions. Equally, one cannot talk of grass-roots activist movements when dealing with the warring factions who issued these posters. In fact the polar distinction between propaganda and activism is further blurred when the posters are analysed in relationship to their audience or perceiving subjects; the different political communities that formed the Lebanese political arena during the war. Based on Crowley and McQuiston's criteria, each political faction can equally denounce the other's posters as deceitful propaganda and claim theirs as rightful political activism.

There is a consensus, it seems, on the understanding of the propaganda poster – as a tool of mass coercion – when it comes to totalitarian regimes and pre-1950s Western state warfare. Outside these specific contexts, it is difficult to find empirical legitimacy for that theoretical model when dealing with political posters in general. It fails to explain the complex role political posters play in the case of a civil war. The success or failure of political posters as tools for mass persuasion and propaganda does not provide satisfactory answers to the questions posed at the beginning of this introduction. If propaganda proceeds from the possibility of closure of meaning in an attempt to exert unilateral control over public opinion, then the posters of Lebanon's civil war attest to the impossibility of absolute closure; a poster can fail to address one person yet communicate effectively with another. That selective communication process is neither arbitrary nor based on the assumption that individuals freely interpret messages communicated in political posters. The model of the propaganda poster, with a persuasive function, does not provide answers to the complexity in which political posters enter into a meaningful communicative exchange with particular political groups.

If we begin to rethink the concept of propaganda and question the models of communication on which its various definitions are built, perhaps we could move beyond the reductive notions of 'mass persuasion', 'coercion' and 'deceit'. We could then undertake a more complex examination of the posters as inscribed in the socio-political institution of political communities during civil war time. In the following sections, I will present the limits of the concept of propaganda and argue for alternative theoretical concepts and models of communication, which will allow me to advance a conceptualization of political posters as symbolic sites of struggle over meaning and political discourse. It's with this premise that I proceed in this book with my study of political posters in Lebanon's civil war.

Rethinking propaganda

Beyond the poster format, the analytic models used to articulate the concept of propaganda in other forms of mass media (television, radio, newspapers, film etc.) have been as controversial within the field of media studies over the past decades. Theoretical ruptures as well as the intense social and political struggles since the 1960s influenced the debates in media and cultural theory. Accordingly, critical scholarship on media in the past decades, grounded primarily within British Cultural Studies, has dropped the term 'propaganda' in favour of alternative concepts based on revised models of communication processes that I shall return to later in this introduction. However, in an attempt to propose new definitions of propaganda adapted to contexts of democracy and liberal politics, the concept of propaganda still persisted among certain scholars. Herman and Chomsky's *Manufacturing Consent: The Political Economy of the Mass Media* is one example of a critical examination of 'propaganda' as it is systematically developed in privately run news media institutions. Herman and Chomsky's study focuses on news coverage and the process through which knowledge and information is produced. Their proposed propaganda model 'traces the routes by which money and power are able to filter out the news fit to print, marginalize dissent, and allow the government and dominant private interests to get their message across to the public'.[7]

Furthermore, Jowett and O'Donnell in their widely read textbook *Propaganda and Persuasion* examine propaganda as an aspect of communication to be differentiated from persuasion and information, yet forming a subcategory of those two forms. Through an expanded study of propaganda in various media, they define propaganda as 'the deliberate, systematic attempt to shape perceptions, manipulate cognitions, and direct behavior to achieve a response that furthers the desired intent of the propagandist'.[8] Even though their definition is similar to the totalitarian-regimes poster definition described above, its applications stretch beyond contexts of repressive systems where media institutions are directly controlled by central state power.

However, their delimitation of the definition to very specific conditions and forms of communication raises some serious doubts on their conception of the communication process. Jowett and O'Donnell distinguish propaganda from other, 'free' forms of communication and knowledge dissemination: 'the elements of deliberate intent and manipulation along with a systematic plan to achieve a purpose that is advantageous to the propagandist . . . distinguish propaganda from a free and open exchange of ideas'.[9] Their statement presupposes that there is a form of media communication that scrupulously lies outside structures of power. It almost suggests that a form of non-propagandistic communication, 'a free and open exchange of ideas', exists outside the control of language and discourse in society. Their focus on 'the deliberate intent of the propagandist' as a defining principle in propaganda ignores the complex processes of communication itself, namely the power structures inherent to the production and circulation of meanings. Communication in their view is 'a process in which a sender transmits a message to a receiver through a channel'.[10] This view framed within a linear transactional model of communication disregards the workings of language, representation and discourse. As will be discussed later, these are inherent to any form of communication, where belief systems and cultural meanings are produced and exchanged. Hence, the form of argumentation proposed by Jowett and O'Donnell does not resolve the theoretical weakness of the concept of propaganda as an empirical construct.

Jowett and O'Donnell acknowledge that meaning is constructed and related to social context yet they maintain that this is an issue the propagandist is very well aware of and employs to his advantage.[11] They note: 'Because so many factors determine the formation of beliefs, attitudes, and behaviors, the propagandist has to gather a great deal of information about the intended audience.'[12] Their definition is thus not only limited to the propagandist's deliberate intentionality but also by his/her exclusion from the 'intended' audience subjected to propaganda. The narrow scope in which such a definition of propaganda can be applied excludes a wide array of media communication where propagandist and audience are both subjects of the same social formation.

The definition presupposes a clean separation between audience and propagandist as social entities to which beliefs and symbolic meanings are attributed. On the one hand, such a scenario disregards the propagandist's own belief system, which affects the 'information about the intended audience': that is, the outlook of the propagandist, as an outsider to the intended audience, constrains his perception of that audience. On the other hand, the audience's beliefs and attitudes are considered positive factual 'information' that precedes the process of propaganda. In other words, Jowett and O'Donnell claim that the propagandist acts on fixed, preconstituted grounds where beliefs and attitudes are clearly defined and quantifiable. Evidently, if the audience is understood to have essential characteristics and fixed beliefs then, by the same token, no change of perceptions can be brought upon them and hence the role of propaganda fails.

Alternatively, if propaganda is seen as a form of communication that instigates change in its audience, then the audience is under constant fluctuations of beliefs and attitudes determined by the various propaganda and 'many factors' that it is exposed to. So the audience can hardly be reduced to a homogeneous entity and summed up into pieces of 'information' even if propagandists might make such a claim. In today's 'media overload' where a multitude of competing mediated discourses are happening simultaneously, it is hard to imagine one single propaganda activity taking place and influencing its audience unaffected by contingencies outside the work of propaganda. In the case of Lebanon's civil war, as mentioned earlier, multiple voices were heard at once without forming, at any point, a harmonious national chorus.

To sum up, the arguments I have raised against Jowett and O'Donnell's definition of propaganda can be outlined by the following three points. First, the process of propaganda cannot be limited to issues of intentionality and clear-cut conceptual separation between propagandist and audience. Second, communication cannot be reduced to a linear transmission process, without examining how meanings and belief systems are written into language and discourse. And third, power in media communication cannot be simply viewed as operating in a unidirectional top-down model of domination – as Stuart Hall puts it, 'it's not like a tap on the knee-cap'. That is, power does not simply emanate from the propagandist onto the audience as he/she manipulates and directs their thinking and behaviour. Rather, power is embedded in the production of knowledge and discourses interchangeably conducted by propagandists and their audience. So propaganda cannot be reduced to a mechanical process of transmission of manipulative messages by a propagandist inducing desired effects on a mass audience. In the following sections, I will introduce an alternative model of media communication by Stuart Hall that critiques the traditional model of propaganda based on message–sender–receiver and considers media communication as a process of 'encoding/decoding'.

Hall's model of 'encoding/decoding'

Stuart Hall's paper 'Encoding/decoding', first published in 1973 and revised in 1980, had a major impact on the research on mass media and is now considered to have set the direction of British Cultural Studies. British Cultural Studies, which began in the 1960s at the Birmingham Centre for Contemporary Cultural Studies, where Hall spent 15 years (1964–79), is a critical interdisciplinary approach to the study of contemporary society.[13] In 'Encoding/decoding', Hall challenged the traditional model of communication in mass media research through a critique of three of its major constituents: the transparency of media message and content, the linearity of the communication process, and the audience's passivity to media manipulation. While I have introduced these issues briefly earlier, I want to elaborate on them in relation to Hall's paper. In what follows, I will expand on the key theoretical constructs of *discourse*, *articulation* and *hegemony* that Hall built his arguments upon. These, together with Hall's model of 'encoding/decoding', form the analytic tools for my study in this book.

Hall's critique of the transparency of media message and content is theoretically grounded in semiotic approaches to language and representation, as well as in Michel Foucault's concept of discourse and the politics of representation. Hall elucidates how meanings are constructed through representational systems, language and images, which function through culturally coded signs. He addresses the complex message of televisual media, constituted by both visual and aural signs, in part a characteristic of posters too. He argues that while images can carry a degree of resemblance to the object being represented, they do not present a fixed unilateral meaning of that object. Representation in media communication, he claims, is the result of a *discursive practice*, on which he writes:

> The dog in the film can bark but it cannot bite! Reality exists outside language, but it is constantly mediated by and through language: and what we can know and say has to be produced in and through discourse. Discursive 'knowledge' is the product not of the transparent representation of the 'real' in language but of the articulation of language on real relations and conditions. Thus there is no intelligible discourse without the operation of a code.[14]

Hall refers in this statement to Foucault's concept of discourse as a representational system – a coherent ensemble of signifying sequences governed by rules of formation and social codes that are historically instituted. Meaning, Foucault claims, is constructed through discourse whereby our knowledge of the 'real' is produced.

Discourse defines and limits ways of talking about a subject as well as the rules of conduct within society at a particular time in history.

Hall equally turns to semiotics to address the general misconceptions on the image as a transparent representation of the 'real'. He holds that while the signs in images are less arbitrary than language/text in their relation to the object signified, 'this does not mean that no codes have intervened; rather, that the codes have been profoundly *naturalized*'.[15] In this statement and subsequent ones, Hall grounds his arguments with Roland Barthes's semiotic study of the photographic image in journalism and advertising. In his analysis of the advertising image, Barthes distinguishes between two types of signification systems: 'The image connoted system – a coded iconic message' and 'the image denoted system – a non-coded iconic message'. He maintains, as does Hall, that the distinction serves the purpose of analysis; it certainly does not occur in ordinary reading since both systems share the same iconic subject matter; 'the viewer of the image receives them *at one and the same time*'.[16]

The connoted system of the image, Barthes claims, articulates a series of discontinuous signs by which meanings are symbolically coded. These signs are culturally, historically and ideologically embedded and require different kinds of knowledge from the viewer. The denoted system of the image, on the other hand, seems literal and perceptual. It consists of a number of identifiable nameable objects present in the scene depicted. The denoted level, Barthes states, constitutes 'a paradox of a message without a code'. The act of naming or referring to these objects in language supposes the intervention of a linguistic code. Barthes identified the denotative aspect of the message in his earlier study 'Myth today' as a 'first order of signification', which he assigns to the system of language. He considers that the first completed meaning or linguistic sign acts as the signifier in a 'second-order system of signification' to refer to meanings and concepts (signifieds) that are the result of social convention and ideology. The second-order signification enters the realm of 'myth', he claims. As an ideological form of discourse, 'myth', according to Barthes, is a '*metalanguage*' that gets hold of language to *naturalize* its own meanings and concepts.[17] As we return to his later study on the advertising image, Barthes restates that the *denoted* aspect in the advertising image masks the constructed meaning (connotation) under a seemingly intrinsic meaning, a 'natural being-there' of the objects represented. He writes: 'the denoted image naturalizes the symbolic message, it innocents the semantic artifice of connotation, which is extremely dense, especially in advertising'.[18]

In Barthes's semiotic analysis, the discontinuous signs or scattered coded meanings, at the connotative level of the image, are unified through a relational *flow* of denotative signs in the image, a 'natural being-there' of the objects in the scene. Through denotation, the various connoted signs add up to a coherent whole, which forms the advertisement discourse around a certain product. The denoted iconic image *naturalizes* the coded, constructed meaning; 'the discontinuous world of symbols', Barthes affirms, 'plunges into the story of the denoted scene as though into a lustral bath of innocence'.[19]

Building on discourse theory and semiotics, Hall argues that messages are *discursively* 'encoded' and 'decoded' at either end of the communication chain. At an initial moment, messages are 'encoded' into 'meaningful discourse', *articulated* within the frameworks of knowledge of the sender/broadcasting institution. At another moment, the message is 'decoded', read as 'meaningful discourse' by the audience within particular frameworks of knowledge. He adds: 'The codes of encoding and decoding may not be perfectly symmetrical'. The degrees of asymmetry in the communication exchange depend on the degrees of symmetry/asymmetry in the frameworks of knowledge, or the discursive difference in the social space, between broadcasters and audiences. This difference, which Hall terms 'lack of fit', is manifested 'between the codes of "source" and "receiver" at the moment of transformation into and out of the discursive form'.[20]

This brings us to his proposed model of the communication process. In order to counter the linear transmission model of sender–message–receiver, Hall builds on Marx's model of commodity production to propose a circuit produced and sustained by *articulated* moments of encoding/production and decoding/consumption. He states the following:

> The value of this approach is that while each of the moments, in articulation, is necessary to the circuit as whole, no one moment can fully guarantee the next moment with which it is articulated. . . . we must recognize that the discursive form of the message has a privileged position in the communicative exchange (from the viewpoint of circulation), and that the moments of 'encoding' and 'decoding', though only 'relatively autonomous' in relation to the communicative process as a whole, are *determinate* moments.[21]

The notion of 'articulation' is recurrent in Hall's texts. He uses it to address the form of linkage that can create a unity in discourse of different and distinct elements – ideological and social forces, which can be rearticulated in different ways in different moments and historical conditions. Articulation is a linkage, Hall claims, that 'is not necessary, determined, absolute and essential for all time'.[22] With that Hall breaks with the economic determinism and necessary class character of the classical Marxist theory of ideological articulation. By framing articulation within a discursive practice, Hall meets post-Marxist perspectives on discourse, particularly that of Ernesto Laclau and Chantal Mouffe's conception of 'discursive articulation'.[23] In their essay 'Beyond the positivity of the social: antagonisms and hegemony', Laclau and Mouffe define articulation in the context of a discursive totality as follows:

> we will call *articulation* any practice establishing a relation among elements such that their identity is modified as a result of the articulatory practice. The structured totality resulting from the articulatory practice, we will call *discourse*. The differential positions, insofar as they appear articulated within a discourse, we will call *moments*. By contrast, we will call *element* any difference that is not discursively articulated.[24]

Their regard to the process of *discursive articulation* derives from three specifications Laclau and Mouffe attribute to discursive formations. The first pertains to the mental and material extent of the discursive formation in including both language and practice. Another specification concerns the coherence of a discursive formation. While being close to Foucault's formulation of 'regularity in dispersion', as a characteristic of coherence within a discursive formation, they are more concerned with *articulated moments* – an ensemble of differential positions in a discursive field.[25] The third aspect, of most relevance to the model of 'encoding/decoding', pertains to the degrees of openness and closure of a discursive formation. Discourse, according to Laclau and Mouffe, conceived within a relational and differential logic, renders the discursive field without any closure, whereby meanings can never be ultimately fixed but extend to an infinite play of signification. Yet they argue that a discursive totality does not occur without any limitation: 'neither absolute fixity nor absolute non-fixity is possible'. The impossibility of absolute closure entails 'partial fixations', otherwise the *articulation* of *elements* into *moments* would not take place.

In light of Laclau and Mouffe's definition of *articulation* within a discursive totality, we can understand Hall's use of 'moments in articulation' in his 'encoding/decoding' model as an assertion of the *partial fixation* of meaning, through his affirmation of the *relational* (relative autonomy), yet *necessary* (determinate) character of the moments in the discursive structure of the communication process. Hall refers to a *partial fixation* of meaning when he examines the differential yet hierarchical character of connotative signs within the social. Codes are the result of a discursive practice that constructs, in Hall's terms, 'dominant or preferred meanings':

> The different areas of social life appear to be mapped out into discursive domains, hierarchically organized into *dominant or preferred meanings*. . . . We say *dominant*, not 'determined', because it is always possible to order, classify, assign and decode an event within more than one 'mapping'. But we say 'dominant' because there exists a pattern

of 'preferred readings'; and these both have the institutional/political/ideological order imprinted in them and have themselves become institutionalized.[26]

Thus, Hall's model of 'encoding/decoding' dispels the closure of meaning or its total fixation by the sender as conceived in traditional models of communication, while simultaneously eliminating the possibility of an endless play of meaning in a process of media communication. Encoding, he claims, does not guarantee decoding, yet Hall maintains that there must be '*some* degree of reciprocity' between those two moments, 'otherwise we could not speak of an effective communicative exchange at all'.[27]

Hall's critique of the ideas of transparency of media content and linearity of message transmission enables him to challenge the third component of the transmission model of communication: audience passivity to media manipulation. Here he links the 'politics of signification' in media discourse with Gramsci's concept of 'hegemonic struggle' to outline three hypothetical positions in audience decoding of televisual discourse: a 'dominant-hegemonic' position whereby both encoding and decoding operate within the hegemony of a dominant discourse; a 'negotiated' decoding that acknowledges the legitimacy of the message discourse but negotiates it within a particular and situated logic; and a third, 'oppositional' position, which resists the dominant discourse of the message and subverts its meanings within alternative discursive frameworks.[28]

Stuart Hall, among other scholars working in the framework of cultural studies, has attached a lot of importance to the concept of hegemony, as outlined by the Italian Marxist Antonio Gramsci. The study of counter-hegemonic cultural practices, as manifested in various forms of socio-political struggle, has had a key role in British Cultural Studies and has radicalized approaches to media studies. The definition of hegemony has shifted historically from that of political rule between states to a Marxist-Leninist conception of 'class alliances'. Gramsci, still within Marxist perspectives, extended hegemony to a process of complex social *struggle*, articulated through political and ideological forces, not determined by class belonging as a pre-constituted identity.[29] In his conception of hegemony, in modern democratic states, power is not expressed in direct political control of a repressive and coercive type. It works through incorporation and continual struggle to win the consent of social groups and maintain dominance. Hegemony, therefore, is a whole social and political process, which permeates cultural meanings, values, beliefs and practices. Raymond Williams, a leading figure in British Cultural Studies, observes that hegemony is neither a passive form of control nor a permanent one; 'It has continually to be renewed, recreated, defended, and modified. It is also continually resisted, limited, altered, challenged by pressures not at all its own.'[30]

Here the understanding of power through hegemony is not far from Foucault's conception of power as 'written into' the production of knowledge and discourses. Yet Foucault frames his conception of discourse against the Marxist notion of 'ideology' as false consciousness. He claims that 'effects of truth' lie within discourses that are in themselves neither true nor false.[31] According to Foucault, truth is linked to power and is inscribed within an authoritative system, a 'regime of truth' which is produced and sustained through discursive formations. Truth, he claims,

> induces regular effects of power. Each society has its regime of truth, its 'general politics' of truth: that is, the types of discourse which it accepts and makes function as true; the mechanisms and instances which enable one to distinguish true and false statements, the means by which each is sanctioned; the techniques and procedures accorded value in the acquisition of truth; the status of those who are charged with saying what counts as true.[32]

Hall's hypothetical position on audience decoding of media messages dispels the conception of audience passivity to media manipulation. It is premised on conceptions of power as outlined in theories of *hegemony* and *discourse*, whereby power is inscribed in the production of discourses that are legitimized or struggled over by social actors depending on their frameworks of knowledge and 'regimes of truth' in which they operate. Hall's model of 'encoding/decoding' in coordination with theories of *discourse*, *articulation* and *hegemony* has enabled scholars in the field of media studies to abandon the traditional concept of propaganda outlined earlier.[33]

Nonetheless, 'propaganda' as a category seems to stick to media processes that are of immediate political character, as in the case of political posters. Yet as argued earlier, the definition of propaganda does not provide satisfactory answers to how political posters work in the context of civil war. The various posters' plural discursive frameworks attest to the impossibility of absolute closure of meaning and unilateral control over 'the masses' claimed by propaganda. The posters also reveal the political factions' continual attempts to dominate the field of discursivity and construct a 'regime of truth', as part of their hegemonic struggle to win the consent of their own communities and maintain dominance. Rethinking the concept of propaganda enables us to overcome the polarity of propaganda/activism in posters and examine instead how political posters are articulated within the respective discursive formations of social agents in the communication process. It lends to a reconceptualization of political posters as *symbolic sites of hegemonic struggle* – where the process of signification, as Hall argues, is linked to that of political struggle, and in Foucault's terms, the politics of signification joins the battle 'around truth'.

Political posters as symbolic sites of struggle

An understanding of *political posters as symbolic sites of hegemonic struggle* is particularly useful in the study of political posters in the context of Lebanon's war. However, the war presents a complex case where various social and political forces have characterized the constructions and transformations of political communities. Here we cannot speak of hegemony in the sense of *a* single dominant discourse (centre), confronted with an oppositional, counter-hegemonic one, as Hall proposes in his hypothetical positions of audience decoding. While I retain his argument against audience passivity to media manipulation, I do not think that the different political communities that formed the Lebanese political arena during the civil war can be hierarchically divided according to hegemonic and counter-hegemonic discourses. We are instead confronted with a fragmentation of the social into a multiplicity of hegemonic formations, each constituting its own 'regime of truth'.

For this, I return to Laclau and Mouffe's theorization of the social as discursive for their subsequent revision of the concept of hegemony. Their argument on the articulated practice of a discursive totality and its partial fixation brings them to address the multiplicity of 'hegemonic articulations' constructing and operating within a given social/political space. Laclau and Mouffe argue against the idea of a single determinable hegemonic centre as a privileged sector in dominance and claim:

> Hegemony is, quite simply, a political type of relation, a form, if one so wishes, of politics; but not a determinable location within a topography of the social. In a given social formation, there can be a variety of hegemonic nodal points.[34]

Their development on the concept of hegemony beyond the notion of a single dominant sector, against which counter-hegemony is formed, is of particular relevance to Lebanon's civil war. As I shall examine in the analysis of posters in the following chapters, Lebanon's political discords are the result of various struggles pertinent to both regional politics and internal socio-political conflicts. The varied social and political forces forming a particular discourse are often linked, for instance socialism with Arab nationalism, class with confessional identity, and confessional belonging with nationalism. The articulated character of a given community's political discourse lends to the partial fixation of its identity and its openness to transformation throughout the war period. Each political community's identity is equally the result of antagonistic relations taking place between the different communities that make up the socio-political space of the Lebanese civil war.[35] The antagonistic relation between discourses constructs, as Laclau and Mouffe define, 'frontier effects' between one hegemonic socio-political identity and another, for instance Arab nationalism vs Lebanese nationalism, Muslim community vs Christian community. Hence a community is imagined as a totality on the basis of its own constructed limits with respect to another. The process does not involve a total fixation of a political identity, nor require an a priori essential identity, for instance on the basis of religion as the conflict has often been narrowly depicted. The antagonistic relation between identities is the result of *hegemonic articulation*; political identities structured through *hegemonic articulations*, as Laclau and Mouffe claim, are not essential, nor fixed. They are not an a priori condition of political conflict but rather constructed, maintained or transformed in and through the work of hegemony, in and through political struggles.

Coupled with the premise posited earlier that political posters act as sites of hegemonic struggle, the theoretical construct of hegemony provides a useful tool of analysis for the case study in this book. Far from being innocent carriers of political activism, or simply coercive tools of propaganda, the political posters are inscribed in the *hegemonic articulations* of political communities in Lebanon's war. The posters articulate the discourses, desires, fears and collective imaginaries pertinent to the various political identities being formed and transformed during wartime.

 The following chapters examine the posters in their contexts of production and circulation and focus on the moments of encoding and message articulation into meaningful discourse in Hall's model. The decoding moment, in the form of direct audience response to the poster message, cannot be the subject of study in this book, since the lapse of time and changes in the socio-political dynamics does not allow such an examination. Yet decoding is not entirely absent from the purview of a study of the posters as artefacts within the civil war's history of events. Furthermore, it is also possible to conceive of the multiplicity of positions vis-à-vis a poster's discourse through a comparative study of the posters. Diverging positions can be examined through a comparative analysis of antagonist and competing discourses, as articulated in the posters of opposing factions.

 The book presents a study of the posters through the analysis of signs and discourses in their textual, visual and aesthetic materializations. The study moves between the semiotic signs of the posters, the political discourse and the historical moment in which the poster message is written. The interpretive analysis of the posters attempts to trace the hegemonic articulations of the multiple political communities. It thus involves situating these posters in their socio-political and historical frameworks. In order to do so, I have resorted to a number of relevant studies on the history of modern Lebanon, the conflicts of the civil war and warring factions, in addition to focused studies on the various political parties and their own published literature. Furthermore, my analysis has greatly benefited from the interviews I have conducted with the authors of posters, media officials of different political parties and printing houses that have closely collaborated with particular political factions in the production of posters.

The book opens with a poster-illustrated chart that provides chronology(ies) of the war events supported with basic information on the major warring factions. The chart allows a multi-layered reading of the war through the posters published by the different parties.

Chapter 1 is concerned with the aesthetic and technical components of poster design and production, which are intrinsic to a poster's encoding. It examines the role of media offices in political parties in the production of political posters and looks into their networks of collaboration with artists/experts. The chapter focuses on the different aesthetic genres of political posters of the civil war by examining the factors that informed the aesthetic layer. It takes into account the agents/authors involved in the design process, their political affiliations and aesthetic approaches, as well as regional and international stylistic influences brought by networks of solidarity and political alliances.

Chapters 2, 3, 4 and 5 respectively address four major themes, recurrent subjects of communication in the posters across the different parties and war phases: Leadership; Commemoration; Martyrdom; Belonging. They study the weight each of these themes has held in the discursive frameworks of Lebanon's civil war and analyse how these dominant themes have been represented. Each chapter allows us to observe the multiple discourses and visual representations around the same theme, providing a more focused comparative discourse analysis and semiotic study of the signs and iconography across the parties.

The book presents a sample of 150 out of a collection of 700 posters that I based my study on. The selection covers a diverse range of posters issued by more than 20 prominent political factions across the different phases of the war. It exemplifies the prevailing political discourses within thematic typologies of posters. The selection is meant to illustrate the analysis and support the arguments I'm presenting in the book.

Graphic
Chronologies

This section presents a chart illustrated by posters that provides chronologies of the war from 1975 to 1990, supported with essential information on the major warring factions. The chart proceeds on two axes, horizontally with a year-by-year unfolding of benchmark events, and vertically across the various parties. It thus allows a multi-layered chronology of the war through the posters published by the different factions. The posters in this chart were chosen from the selection of posters discussed in the book based on two intersecting criteria: the portrayal of a major event in the war and the representation of a particular party across the years of the war. All the posters in the following chart appear later in the book in larger size with the corresponding details. For instance, 2.5 indicates the 5th figure in chapter 2.

Lebanese Kataeb Party

Lebanese Front

Tanzim

Lebanese Forces

→

Lebanese National Movement

Palestinian Liberation Organization in Lebanon

Progressive Socialist Party

→

Lebanese Communist Party

Organization of Communist Action in Lebanon

→

Syrian Social Nationalist Party

Nasserist movements

Arab Socialist Baath Party

→

Amal movement

Hizbullah

→

4.23

5.14

5.1

3.15

3.17

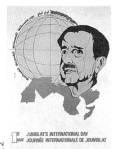

2.2

2.5

4.22

1.21

5.12

5.4

3.26

3.11

2.19

5.15 ...ومنعتر بالّي بيبقوا !!!

3.4 ٤٤ سنة في خدمة لبنان

2.16

5.19

5.17

5.9

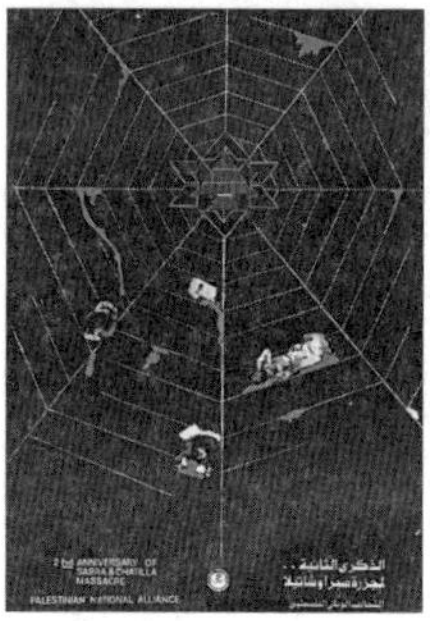

3.20

4.26

4.24

1.8

1.16

5.18

4.29

2.20

1.32

1983

2.15

1984

5.22

1985

1986

4.18

5.25

2.12

3.6

4.12

4.20

3.16

4.31

4.21

3.22

2.22

4.38

2.7 الذكرى العاشرة لاستشهاد كمال جنبلاط ١٩١٧ـ١٩٧٧

3.24

4.25

4.41

Warring fronts and political parties

Lebanese Front

The Lebanese Front was a coalition formed on the eve of the civil war, consisting of leaders of the dominant Christian Maronite establishment and right-wing Lebanese nationalist parties with their affiliated military organizations. It was presided over by Camil Chamoun (NLP); its leadership included Pierre Gemayel (LKP), Suleiman Frangieh (president of Lebanon 1970–6) and other notable Maronite political, religious and intellectual figures. The leaders comprising the front favoured a neutral position of Lebanon with regards to the Arab–Israeli conflict. The front joined forces against the armed presence of Palestinian organizations in Lebanon, regarding the PLO as a threat to Lebanon's peace and sovereignty. The front was equally sceptical of Arab nationalism and strongly opposed left-wing proposed reforms. Its affiliated military organizations formed a joint military command in 1976 under the name of the Lebanese Forces.

Lebanese Kataeb Party (LKP) or Phalange

Pierre Gemayel who led the Kataeb until his death in 1984 founded the party in 1936. It is a right-wing Lebanese nationalist party; its partisans are essentially Christian, mostly Maronite. The Kataeb was a central member of the Lebanese Front coalition. Gemayel's two sons, Amin and Bashir, played key roles in the party's politics and military organization, respectively. Bashir Gemayel was elected president of Lebanon in 1982; assassinated shortly after, he was succeeded by his brother Amin.

National Liberal Party (NLP)

Founded in 1958 by Camil Chamoun, the NLP was a right-wing Lebanese nationalist party. The party held a predominantly Christian membership with pro-Western political views and anti-Arab-nationalism sentiments. Chamoun was the president of the Lebanese Front alliance, while his son Dani commanded the NLP's military arm, the Numur (Tigers).

With the rise of Bashir Gemayel's command over the Lebanese Forces, the Numur's military power was forcefully terminated through violent battles in 1980. A significant number of the Numur partisans were absorbed into the ranks of the Lebanese Forces.

Tanzim

A small organization formed in 1969 by former members of the Kataeb party, George Adwan, Fouad Chemali and Fawzi Mahfouz, who were radically opposed to the presence of Palestinian forces in Lebanon. The organization held an important position within the Lebanese Front coalition and played a substantial military role. In 1977 the Tanzim split in two and the wing led by Mahfouz merged with the Lebanese Forces.

Guardians of the Cedars

A political movement and military organization established in 1975 on the eve of the war, led by a former police officer, Etienne Sakr (Abu Arz). Right-wing, ultra-Lebanese-nationalist and hostile to Arabism, it called for the expulsion of Palestinian refugees and forces from Lebanon. The organization fought as part of the Lebanese Forces in the early years of the war. In the mid-1980s, it fought alongside the Israeli army in South Lebanon against the Palestinian forces and the Lebanese National Resistance Front.

Marada

A political movement formed by Suleiman Frangieh during his presidency (1970–6). Frangieh's son, Tony, commanded the Marada's military wing. Partisans are Maronites from the North Lebanon region of Zghorta. It fought alongside the Lebanese Front in the north between 1975 and 1976. However, Suleiman Frangieh's close relationship to Syria, his accusations that the other members of the front were cooperating with Israel, and the subsequent murder of Tony Frangieh by the Kataeb in 1978 led the Marada movement to rupture its alliance with the Lebanese Front.

Lebanese Forces (LF)

The Lebanese Forces were established in 1976, initially as a joint military command for the Lebanese Front coalition. It grouped the military organizations of four predominant parties: the Kataeb party, the National Liberal Party's Numur, the Guardians of the Cedars and the Tanzim. Bashir Gemayel commanded the Lebanese Forces, in collaboration with the military leaders of the parties involved. In 1980 Bashir Gemayel launched an offensive against Dani Chamoun's Numur, terminating its military power. Gemayel gained exclusive command of the Lebanese Forces and military control over Beirut's eastern sectors, as the military structures of the rest of the political groups were absorbed into its ranks. The Lebanese Forces grew into a formidable military structure benefiting from the support of Israel and the backing of other political powers. The Lebanese Forces in 1985, under Elie Hobeika and Samir Geagea, staged a coup to gain political governance independent from the Kataeb and Amin Gemayel's rule. This was followed by a second uprising in 1986, against Hobeika's accommodating relation with Syria, bringing Geagea to power.

Lebanese National Movement (LNM)

The Lebanese National Movement was large and heterogeneous; it grouped leftist and national parties and was headed by Kamal Jumblatt. It was initiated in 1969 under the name of the Front of National and Progressive Parties. The movement strove for socio-political reforms that challenged national economic policies, the confessional system and the Maronite dominance of Lebanon's political system. The movement favoured Lebanon's active involvement in the Arab–Israeli conflict and supported the Palestinian resistance in its liberation struggle. During wartime, the combined forces of the LNM operated in conjunction with the PLO's different military factions. In 1976 Syria's intervention in Lebanon and its political discord with the LNM and PLO caused parties aligned with Syria to split from the LNM and forge an alliance under the name of the Front of Patriotic and National Parties. The assassination of Kamal Jumblatt in 1977 and Syria's control of the Lebanese political scene weakened the movement. Finally, the Israeli invasion in 1982 and the evacuation of the PLO forces contributed to the dissolution of the National Movement.

Lebanese National Resistance Front (LNRF)

Following the Israeli invasion, the Lebanese National Resistance Front was created on 16 September 1982 at the initiative of the Lebanese Communist Party and the Organization of Communist Action. The front formalized the resistance activities of those parties, as well as the Syrian Social Nationalist Party and other members of the Front of Patriotic and National Parties.

Palestinian Liberation Organization in Lebanon (PLO)

Operating under the Palestinian Liberation Organization, the Palestinian resistance grouped a number of organizations with varied ideologies, each with its own leadership and military apparatus: Fatah, Popular Front for the Liberation of Palestine (PFLP), Democratic Front for the Liberation of Palestine (DFLP), Arab Liberation Front, as-Sa'iqa, PFLP – General Command, and the Palestine Liberation Army, the official military arm of the PLO.

In 1969 an agreement signed in Cairo between the Lebanese army and the PLO officially permitted Palestinian resistance while constraining it to Lebanon's southern border. Following the expulsion of the PLO from Jordan in 1970, the organization moved its headquarters to Lebanon. South Lebanon became an important base for military operations on the border with Israel. The resistance organizations benefited from the political support of left-wing and Arab nationalist parties and held Lebanese partisans among their ranks.

The PLO was a major actor in the war as it supported the combined forces of the LNM on many levels, lending financial support, military resources and training. Military factions of the PLO participated – unofficially – in the war fronts. However, Syria's intervention in Lebanon in 1976 and its pronounced discord with the PLO produced a different political set-up that rendered the PLO openly active in the armed conflict. Following the 1982 Israeli invasion, the PLO forces were evacuated from Beirut under the supervision of multinational forces.

Progressive Socialist Party (PSP)

Founded in 1949 and led by Kamal Jumblatt, a descendant of a Druze feudal family of the Shouf Mountains. Jumblatt played a key role in civil war politics, since he presided over the National Movement. Jumblatt contested Syria's intervention in 1976; he denounced its plan to prevent an imminent victory of the LNM and weaken the Palestinian resistance. Jumblatt was assassinated on 16 March 1977. In the same year Walid, Kamal Jumblatt's son, who succeeded his father in leadership of the party and the LNM, issued a common statement with the pro-Syrian Baath party and began to reconcile the PSP with the Patriotic Front and Syria. Despite secular beginnings and progressive programmes, the PSP came to represent a continuation of the Jumblatt family's traditional leadership over the Druze sect when Walid Jumblatt assumed leadership. The party's Druze identity got further pronounced as it engaged in Druze–Christian inter-communitarian violence during the 1982–4 mountain battles with the Lebanese Forces.

Lebanese Communist Party (LCP)

It was founded in 1924 as the Communist Party of Syria and Lebanon, remaining so until 1944 when independent parties were established in each country. Its membership is multi-confessional; it grouped a large body of intellectuals and workers among its ranks. The LCP featured significantly in the National Movement and participated actively in the war front from 1975. In 1982 it formed the Lebanese National Resistance Front with other parties, and led major military operations against the Israeli occupation. The party suffered from the assassination of some of its prominent members throughout the course of the war.

Organization of Communist Action in Lebanon (OCA)

Founded in 1970 as a union between two radical-left movements, the OCA was an independent organization that adopted Marxist-Leninist thought. It represented the new left with an overwhelmingly youth multi-confessional membership that was inspired by the revolutionary struggles and protest movements of the late 1960s. It played an important role in the war politics, as its leader Mohsen Ibrahim was the executive secretary of the National Movement. Its military forces actively engaged on the war front and particularly in joined operations with the Palestinian forces in the south. The organization partook in the formation of the Lebanese National Resistance Front.

Syrian Social Nationalist Party (SSNP)

Founded in 1932 by Antun Saadeh, the SSNP held the objective of resuscitating historic Greater Syria as a unified social and geographic national entity. The party grew considerably and had multi-sectarian membership. Saadeh was executed by the Lebanese state in 1949, accused of an attempted coup d'état. The SSNP fought on many fronts alongside the LNM and the PLO in 1975 and 1976. With Syria's intervention in 1976 and rising tensions between LNM–PLO and Syria, the party's internal political divisions were aggravated. It suffered defections, forming a separate faction aligned with Syria. The party actively participated from 1982 in the National Resistance Front and undertook many military operations against Israeli occupation in Beirut and South Lebanon. The SSNP's resistance endeavours were halted in 1987 with the ascendancy of the Islamic Resistance coupled with heightened internal discords in the party leadership and politics of alliance with Syria.

Nasserist movements

Independent Nasserist Movement – Murabitun (INM): Formed in 1958 and led by Ibrahim Koleilat, the Murabitun embraced the pan-Arab nationalist and Socialist projects of the Egyptian president Gamal Abd-el-Nasser and was a firm supporter of the Palestinian resistance. Al-Murabitun, the movement's military wing, played a major part during the civil war, fighting among the combined forces of the LNM. Most of its members were Sunni Muslim. In 1985 the Progressive Socialist Party and Amal joined forces to suppress the Murabitun and forced Koleilat into exile.

Socialist Arab Union: Its formation in Lebanon dates back to the early 1970s as a Nasserist movement tied to the Socialist Arab Union in Egypt. In 1975 the movement split into two factions, both of which were active in the LNM.

Other smaller Nasserist movements were equally active in Lebanon and partook in the civil war: the Popular Nasserist Organization, based in Saida, led by Maarouf Saad and subsequently his two sons; and the Union of Toiling Peoples' Forces, based in west Beirut and led by Kamal Shatila.

Arab Socialist Baath Party

Founded in 1947 in Syria, the Baath was premised on Arab national unity, and later embraced socialism. Early on, the party expanded its scope of activities into Jordan, Lebanon and Iraq and supported liberation struggles in the Arab world. The Baath seized power in Syria and Iraq in 1963, following military coups. The party witnessed internal conflicts in the sixties, which led to divisions between the Syrian and Iraqi Baaths. The schism was reflected upon the Baath party in Lebanon, leading to its division into two wings, a pro-Syrian wing led by Assem Kanso and a pro-Iraqi wing led by Abd-el-Majid al-Rafi'i.

Both wings adhered to the LNM until Syria's intervention in 1976 caused the pro-Syrian Baath to rupture its alliance with the LNM and form the backbone of the Patriotic Front. A common statement issued by the pro-Syrian Baath and the Progressive Socialist Party in 1977, following the assassination of Kamal Jumblatt, led to the reconciliation of Walid Jumblatt, who assumed leadership of the PSP and LNM, with the Patriotic Front and Syria.

Amal movement

Amal means 'Hope' and is the acronym for Afwaj al-Muqawama al-Lubnaniya (Lebanese Resistance Detachments), a movement established in 1975 by the Shi'ite cleric Imam Mussa al-Sadr, as the military arm of the Movement of the Disinherited, which he had founded a year earlier. Al-Sadr advocated socio-political reform and called for social equality for the deprived communities in underdeveloped areas in South Lebanon and the Bekaa. Although officially secular, Amal's membership is overwhelmingly Shi'ite. The movement has worked to mobilize the Shi'ite community around an articulated struggle of confession and class. Al-Sadr disappeared in 1978 during a visit to Libya; he was succeeded by Hussein el-Husseini until Nabih Berri took charge in 1980. Amal did not participate in the 1975–6 fighting; it adhered to the Patriotic Front and endorsed Syria's intervention in 1976. While it officially supports the Palestinian cause in its liberation struggle, Amal repeatedly clashed with the PLO forces in Beirut and southern Lebanon during the 1980s; yet, despite its continuous clashes in west Beirut with other parties (Murabitun, PSP and Hizbullah), Amal also took part in the resistance against Israel in South Lebanon.

Hizbullah

Formed in 1982 at the initiative of a group of Shi'ite clerics who split from the Amal movement, drawn by the Islamic revolution in Iran, and who adhered to the jurisprudence of Khomeini (*Wali al-Faqih*). Hizbullah ('party of God') received Iranian support, which helped establish the party's military infrastructure and institutional development. Hizbullah was officially proclaimed in 1984; it announced the party's active participation in the resistance to Israeli occupation through its military arm, the Islamic Resistance. Hizbullah conceive of their military role as a 'defensive jihad' against oppressors of the *Umma* (Muslim community), taking as a model the martyrdom of Imam Hussein in Karbala (AD 680). The Shi'ite narrative of the Karbala event, commemorated annually through the holiday of Ashura, has marked and informed a Shi'ite revolutionary discourse in Iran and largely inspired the politico-religious ideology of Hizbullah. As the party's growth posed a threat to Israel, its main leaders have repeatedly been targets of Israeli assassinations, among them the founding member Sheikh Ragheb Harb (1984) and the party's secretary-general Abbas Mussawi (1991).

Chronology of wartime events

1975

26 Feb: Lebanese army clashes with labour demonstrators in Saida; leader of the Popular
Nasserist Organization, Maarouf Saad, is
wounded, dying on 6 March

13 Apr: Armed partisans of the Kataeb party attack a bus carrying Palestinian passengers
across Ain el-Rummaneh, east of Beirut,
killing about 33 passengers
The incident triggers violent clashes, and
marks the official beginning of the civil war

Apr: Fighting erupts on different fronts in North
and South Lebanon and Beirut

6 Dec: 'Black Saturday': approximately 200
Muslims killed in Beirut, in revenge for the
killings of four Kataeb members

Dec: Fierce battles over the hotels district in
central Beirut begin

1976

Jan: The siege of several Palestinian refugee
camps situated around the Christian sectors of east Beirut
The Lebanese army begins to disintegrate
into different factions
Fall of the Maslakh and Qarantina in east
Beirut, where indiscriminate killing of residents occurs
Reprisal violence in Christian villages south
of Beirut (Damour); these eventually fall to
the Palestinian and combined forces of the
National Movement

Christian Maronite political leaders insti-
tutionalize their cooperation through the
Lebanese Front

22 Mar: Fall of the Holiday Inn hotel following violent battles, the Lebanese Front loses its last
stronghold in the western sector of Beirut

8 May: Elias Sarkis elected president of Lebanon

June: Syrian army officially enters Lebanon at the
request of President Frangieh and consent
of the Lebanese Front; the deployment of
the Syrian troops is met with resistance by
factions of the National Movement

25 July: Syrian president Hafez al-Assad condemns
the National Movement and PLO in a notorious public speech

Aug: The Lebanese Forces, a unified military arm
of the Lebanese Front, are formed under the
command of Bashir Gemayel

12 Aug: Fall of Tall al-Za'tar Palestinian camp – the
last remaining in east Beirut – to the
Lebanese Front

Nov: Arrival of Arab Deterrent Force (ADF) in
Lebanon, dispatched upon resolutions
taken by the Arab League, and formally ending the two-year civil war; the Syrian troops
form the majority of the ADF

1977

16 Mar: Kamal Jumblatt, Progressive Socialist Party
and Lebanese National Movement leader, is
assassinated

12 Sep: Progressive Socialist Party and pro-Syrian
Baath party in Lebanon proclaim in a common statement a unified Patriotic Front

19 Nov: Egyptian president Anwar el-Sadat visits
Jerusalem as a step towards peace negotiations with Israel

1978

Feb: Clashes between Syrian troops and the
         Lebanese army

14 Mar: 'Operation Litani': Israel invades South
         Lebanon and establishes a buffer zone un-
         der the command of Major Saad Haddad,
         who had defected from the Lebanese army

13 June: Commander of Marada military forces Tony
         Frangieh and his family are murdered dur-
         ing an attack of the Kataeb forces on his
         residence in Ehden

23 June: Based on resolution 425 the United Nations
         Interim Force in Lebanon (UNIFIL) takes up
         positions in the south

July: '100 days' battle between the Lebanese
         Forces and Syrian army; Syrian artillery
         heavily shells the eastern sectors of Beirut

31 Aug: Imam Mussa al-Sadr, founder of Amal
         movement, disappears during a visit to
         Libya

Sep: Camp David Accords signed between Egypt
         and Israel

1979

         Clashes between the Syrian army and
         Lebanese Forces continue

         Israel launches air raids on South Lebanon

Feb: Islamic revolution in Iran brings down the
         Shah's regime

Mar: Saudi Arabia quits the ADF, other members
         follow suit, while Syrian troops remain in
         Lebanon

26 Mar: The Israeli–Egyptian peace treaty is signed

1980

         Israeli raids on South Lebanon continue

July: Bashir Gemayel launches offensive on the
         National Liberal Party militia – Numur –
         and gains exclusive military command of
         the Lebanese Forces and the eastern sectors

1981

         Israel intensifies bombing of South
         Lebanon and raids west Beirut

         PLO and National Movement combined
         forces engage in cross-border operations
         into Israel

2 Mar: Beginning of the Lebanese Forces–Syrian
         battle of Zahleh in the Bekaa

Apr: Confrontation between Syria and Israel in
         the Bekaa leads to a 'missile crisis', subdued
         by US mediation

1982

6 June: Israel invades Lebanon, followed by heavy
         bombardment and a siege of west Beirut

23 Aug: Bashir Gemayel elected president of
         Lebanon

Aug: Syrian troops retreat to North Lebanon and
         the Bekaa

         US–multinational forces arrive in Beirut to
         oversee the evacuation of PLO troops

14 Sep: Assassination of Bashir Gemayel

15 Sep: Israeli army invades Beirut

15–17 Sep: Massacres in Sabra and Shatila Palestinian
         camps in the southern suburbs of Beirut

16 Sep: Left-wing parties form the Lebanese
         National Resistance Front and launch
         operations against Israeli occupation

21 Sep: Amin Gemayel elected president of Lebanon

29 Sep: Israeli army leaves Beirut

Nov: Battles erupt in the mountains (Aley) between the Progressive Socialist Party and the Lebanese Forces

1983

Israel withdraws from the mountains to north of Saida

17 May: The USA brokers an agreement between Israel and Lebanon known as the 'May 17 Accord'

Sep: Large-scale 'mountain war' between the Progressive Socialist Party and Lebanese Forces culminates in Druze vs Christian intercommunitarian violence; PSP seizes southern mountain villages, causing a heavy displacement of Christian communities

23 Oct: Bombing of French and US barracks in Beirut

31 Oct: Inter-Lebanese reconciliation conference at Geneva

Nov: Syrian-backed attacks on Arafat's PLO forces in Tripoli

Dec: Evacuation of Arafat and PLO forces from Tripoli

1984

6 Feb: The forces of Amal movement–Progressive Socialist Party–Syrian Social Nationalist Party lead military offensive against the Lebanese army and seize west Beirut

Feb: Multinational forces withdraw from Lebanon

5 Mar: The Lebanese government annuls 'May 17 Accord' with Israel

12 Mar: Second Lebanese reconciliation meeting in Lausanne

1985

The National Resistance Front intensifies its operations against Israeli occupation

12 Mar: Uprising of the Lebanese Forces led by Hobeika and Geagea against Gemayel's rule, and subsequent Lebanese Forces split from the Kataeb

Mar: Violent confrontations between different militias in west Beirut; Amal movement–Progressive Socialist Party wipe out the Murabitun

May: 'War of the camps': Amal forces besiege Palestinian camps in west Beirut and southern Lebanon

June: Israel retreats from Saida further south to the Litani river

Nov: Fighting between Amal movement and Progressive Socialist Party in west Beirut

28 Dec: Syrian-sponsored tripartite agreement is held between leaders of the Lebanese Forces, Amal movement and Progressive Socialist Party

1986

Continued fighting between Progressive Socialist Party and Amal movement

15 Jan: Second uprising in the Lebanese Forces; Geagea takes command, ousts Hobeika and annuls tripartite agreement

1987

Feb: Syrian troops re-enter west Beirut upon the request of political authorities to suppress militia confrontations

1 June: Assassination of Prime Minister Rashid Karami

1988

May: Clashes between Amal movement and Hizbullah in Beirut southern suburbs

22 Sep: Following the end of his presidential term, Amin Gemayel appoints army general Michel Aoun to head a military government; Muslim authorities disapprove and establish a rival government headed by Salim el-Hoss

1989

Feb: First clashes between Lebanese army commanded by General Aoun and the Lebanese Forces

14 Mar: General Aoun launches 'War of Liberation' against Syrian troops in Lebanon

Sep: Ceasefire called for by the Arab League comes into effect

Oct: The Lebanese parliament meets in Taef, Saudi Arabia, and negotiates an accord to end the conflict

Nov: René Moawad, elected president of Lebanon, is assassinated; shortly after, parliament elects Elias Hrawi president; Aoun denies the legitimacy of Hrawi

1990

31 Jan: Fierce war erupts between the Lebanese Forces and the Lebanese army commanded by General Aoun in east Beirut

Aug: Iraq invades Kuwait, leading to the first Gulf War; Syria cooperates with the US-driven coalition

13 Oct: Syrian army besieges the presidential palace in Baabda; Aoun takes refuge in the French embassy

21 Oct: Commander of the Numur Dani Chamoun and his family are murdered

Nov: Based on the Taef agreement, the Lebanese government proclaims the end of the civil war; the demilitarization of militias begins under the supervision of Syria

1

Agents, Aesthetic Genres
and Localities

Unlike various aesthetic genres of political posters in world history – Soviet socialist realism, Nazi realism, Cuban solidarity posters, among others – the political posters of Lebanon's civil war did not make up a uniform national aesthetic genre that is specific to the country and the event of the war. An evident factor is the absence of a single hegemonic voice and state media apparatus in which a unified political poster genre could develop – a typical scenario to post-revolutions and state warfare in which known poster styles have emerged. The civil war in Lebanon witnessed instead multiple factions of distinct political communities with their respective parties acting as each community's official voice and operating their own media offices. The parties' different ideological frameworks and alliance to diverse regional and international political powers have materialized in equally disparate graphic vocabularies. The lack of a single hegemonic centre and consensus over a national identity can be traced at the level of the aesthetic fragmentation of the posters. For the aesthetic component of the poster is a code that forms an inseparable part of the overall message discourse.

Besides the fact that we cannot claim a unified political poster genre intrinsic to Lebanon, it is also misleading to assume that the civil war constituted a break with pre-existing aesthetic practices in the local visual culture or initiated new aesthetic movements. This, of course, does not overlook the fact that political posters were significantly abundant between 1975 and 1990 and that the discourses and iconography were undeniably linked to the rising conflicts and construction of political identities (as will be discussed at length in the next four chapters). At the level of the aesthetic form however, the political posters have in fact built on the different contemporary visual practices in Lebanon and the Arab region, ranging from Modern painting, book illustration and political cartoon to popular film hoardings. These practices have set the predominant aesthetic typologies of Lebanon's civil war posters. So the posters are aesthetically informed by the professional practices of their authors, as well as networks of collaboration and political alliances between Lebanese political factions and other regional and international political movements.

This chapter provides an analytic study of the prevailing aesthetic genres of political posters during wartime Lebanon and will be divided accordingly. While identifying the characteristics of each genre, I will be addressing the professional practice and individual aesthetic styles of some key poster authors, their affiliation to a certain political struggle, as well as regional and international aesthetic influences on their poster undertaking. Before moving into the aesthetic genres, I will first address the role of media offices in political parties to examine their agency in the production and aesthetic materialization of political posters.

The role of media offices in political parties

The media offices in the majority of Lebanese parties were mostly concerned with the party's publications, newspapers, periodicals and other party literature.[1] The parties did not set up visual arts departments, or engage experts in that area full-time. The media officials of the Lebanese parties were mostly journalists or intellectuals, members of the political bureau, normally eloquent writers, at home with the party's discourse and literature. Nonetheless, their responsibilities involved the issuing of posters among other party publications.[2] All too often, the media official acted as the copywriter, writing the text or slogan, and handled the art direction of the posters. This explains, in part, the abundance of the calligraphy-based posters during the civil war and the primacy of text in political posters in general – politically loaded rhetoric, eloquent slogans, quotations from the party founder or contemporary poets as well as references to classical Arabic poetry.

The calligraphy-centred poster in Lebanon and the Arab world is a continuation of an old practice through new means of production. Words and Arabic calligraphy have historically been engrained in the street culture and architectural landscape of Arab cities. Whether in the form of Koranic verses that ornament the façades of mosques, mansions and symbolic buildings, or in modern times the public banner, *yafta*,[3] mounted in the streets to voice public political commentary, the calligraphic word has had its symbolic, communicative and aesthetic potency in the public domain. The *yafta* in the Arab world preceded the poster as a modern means for the public dissemination of political messages, and occupied the streets at moments of popular uprising and political campaigning. Its value lies in the primacy of the word in public expression and in attributing aesthetic quality to calligraphy, which would vary in style and formal complexity according to the type of message. It hence formed an intrinsic component of the street vernacular of major Arab cities since the first decades of the twentieth century. The calligraphic poster in Lebanon followed similar principles to the *yafta*, in calligraphic style and type of message. In its limited size and large print run, it came to be a commonly adopted poster genre during the civil war, easily and cheaply published by the party.

The process of art direction of posters by media officials involved commissioning specialist calligraphers and illustrators to render their ideas visually, or too often just getting these directly executed at an affiliated printing press. The majority of parties did not own printing presses but instead held close working relationships particularly with those affiliated to the party, near their headquarters, or in the areas they had political and military control over. Some establishments became the 'official' printers of a certain party. Raidy Printing Press, being an established press in the predominantly Christian eastern sector of Beirut and located nearby the Kataeb headquarters, printed most of the Kataeb party and Lebanese Forces publications. On the other hand Techno Press, another major printing establishment, which relocated to west Beirut during the civil war, did work for a variety of leftist parties active in the western sector of the city – the Palestinian organizations, the Progressive Socialist Party and the Lebanese Communist Party. It provided services free of charge for the latter, as the owner of the press and most of its workers were active members of the Lebanese Communist Party.

The posters that the media official executed at the printing press form the larger part of the civil war posters, which were produced under time pressure and conditions of limited communication and mobility during the war. These would usually follow basic layouts and standard templates in their composition, repetitively applied for recurrent subjects. These standardized poster formats were most commonly applied in posters based on portraits of martyrs and political leaders. The central image would be a photographic portrait, accompanied by typical party slogans and related information (see figs in chapters 2 and 4).

Conversely, on special occasions – party anniversary, a political leader's death/assassination or other significant commemorative events – an artist would be called upon to volunteer his/her artwork for a poster. That depended on the party's own network of affiliation with artists in Lebanon and contemporary artists' political commitment, which will be addressed in the following sections.

Political fervour among left-wing Arab artists

The posters of the Palestinian resistance filled the walls of cities in Lebanon from the late 1960s onwards and were a precursor to political posters of the Lebanese civil war. The former presented a model in terms of aesthetic genres, shared revolutionary discourse and iconography pertaining to armed struggle and popular resistance. This was particular to the Lebanese left-wing and Arab nationalist parties, allied with the Palestinian organizations and fighting on the same front. The alliance between the Lebanese National Movement (LNM) and Palestinian organizations forged networks of media and artistic collaboration, whereby a number of artists designed posters for both the Palestinian resistance and the Lebanese parties to which they were affiliated. This makes it difficult to dissociate the aesthetic approaches of Lebanese left-wing political posters from those centred on the Palestinian struggle. In what follows I will discuss the context (political and aesthetic) in which Arab political posters emerged while focusing on examples of artists and posters that directly relate to the Lebanese civil war.

Following the devastating military defeat of Arab states against Israel in 1967, Lebanon among other Arab countries witnessed the rise of Palestinian resistance movements. The struggle for the liberation of a lost homeland that the various movements engaged in was coupled with relentless efforts in organized media activity to advocate the Palestinian cause. The media office of the Palestinian Liberation Organization, based in Beirut, acted as the Unified Information Office and included a fine arts department that catered for the art-related activities of the organization, including the publishing of posters. However it did not hinder poster publishing by other Palestinian organizations and civil movements or by independent Arab and international artists. Posters, among other means, played a key role in awakening or maintaining national identity and mobilizing the youth to actively partake in the resistance, as well as calling for international solidarity with the Palestinian people in their struggle for liberation and social justice.

As the Palestinian Liberation Organization (PLO) relocated from Jordan to Beirut in the early 1970s, it found local support and enthusiasm among the Lebanese left: allied Lebanese political parties, artists and intellectuals, in addition to a fervour among radical youth movements of the time. Meanwhile, Beirut in the sixties was living its heyday as the cosmopolitan centre of the Arab world. The city enchanted businessmen, tourists, artists and intellectuals from the region to partake in its adventure of modernity. This, with a thriving scene in the arts and culture – international music festivals, burgeoning art galleries, venues for alternative theatre productions, in addition to vigorous publishing houses and Arabic book fairs enjoying the intellectual freedom that neighbouring Arab countries at the time lacked – set Beirut in the 1960s as the cultural centre of the Arab world. While the 'Paris of the East' thrilled its dwellers and visitors with a booming economy and assimilation of Western models of consumerism and modern lifestyles, a large segment of the Lebanese population was publicly voicing its economic deprivation and demanding political and social reforms. Describing the rising social movements, strikes and demonstrations that swept the country at the time, Fawwaz Traboulsi notes: 'Much more than a protest movement, it was a radical questioning of Lebanese and Arab societies from a moral and cultural point of view, greatly influenced by the defeat of June 1967, the emergence of the Palestinian resistance and the impact of May 1968 in France.'[4]

The artistic climate in Beirut and other Arab cities, coupled with heightened politicization, created a fertile ground for the development of political posters. Politically engaged artists saw in the poster a public platform to voice their positions and an expansion of their artistic practice from the confines of the galleries to the openness of the city walls. Many prominent Arab artists – Palestinian, Lebanese, Syrian, Iraqi and Egyptian, among others – contributed with great ardency to the design of political posters and advanced distinctive aesthetic standards. Political posters advocating the Palestinian cause have been part of a thriving movement of political engagement through art that called for Arab artists', film-makers' and intellectuals' participation in the socio-political struggles of the region: liberation movements, Arab nationalism, class struggle and opposition to different forms of social injustice.[5] This unprecedented active participation brought esteem to posters as an art form, manifested in institutional support such as international competitions, exhibitions and publications. It started with an exhibition organized by the PLO Unified Information Office with the title *International Exhibition for Palestine*, held at the Beirut Arab University in March 1978, followed the next year by a second in the same location, called *Exhibition of Palestinian Posters 1967–1979*.

Among the Arab countries, Iraq had been the forerunner in advancing the poster as a legitimate art form in the 1970s, by holding state-endorsed poster exhibitions and through the participation in international poster biennales of some of the leading modern Iraqi artists of the period. Among these is Dia' al-Azzawi who besides his participation in the design of posters and organization of exhibitions also wrote a book in 1974, probably the first of its kind in the Arab world, entitled *The Art of Posters in Iraq, a study of its beginning and development 1938–1973*.[6] The Iraqis continued to be active on that front and organized in 1979 the *Baghdad International Poster Exhibition* including a juried international poster competition centred on two themes: 'The third-world struggle for liberation' and 'Palestine, a homeland denied'.

In the absence of academic training in graphic design at the time in Lebanon, it was the formally trained artists, mostly renowned ones, who took the lead in the design of political posters. Generally, prominent modern artists in Lebanon contributed mostly to left-wing and Arab nationalist political parties coalescing under the LNM. This was consistent with the movement of political activism among Arab artists in the late 1960s. As addressed above, the political fervour had materialized early on in posters calling for solidarity with the Palestinian cause, which eventually forged the way for artists' engagement in designing political posters during the Lebanese civil war.

The artists' contributions were sporadic and did not form a steady flow of poster production that could get institutionalized into the Lebanese parties' media framework. The poster artwork was mostly on a volunteer basis and came subsidiary to their main artistic practices, which established artists tried to maintain throughout the war. The poster was generally conceived as an act of political struggle and commitment to a cause through art rather than a professional service, as described by many of the artists and media officials. Additionally, as the connections were ruptured between the various Lebanese communities during the war, the contact between artists and parties was not always an easy process. Some artists maintained unofficial affiliations to parties and opted for anonymous poster contributions in order not to jeopardize their social and professional relations. More so, as the party militias got more involved in violent reprisals and confessional hostilities through the unfolding of the war, many artists discontinued their party affiliation.

The left-wing political posters in Lebanon did not hold a unified aesthetic genre. As with the Palestinian posters, each artist contributed with an already established style of his/her own. The artists' posters were aesthetically as diversified as their authors' painterly approaches. The poster was too often conceived as an aesthetically complex painting. Quite typically, a painting or drawing would be made by the artist before it was adapted into a poster, whereby the text would be sidelined to the author's artwork. Essentially, the artists in most part did not really dwell on the design process of a poster but rather offered their artwork to be published in a poster format. Artists developed posters based on their own artistic preoccupations, which in many cases incorporated their political concerns, not only in the subject matter but also at the level of the visual form. These artistic explorations were contemporaneous with a general undercurrent of modern art in the Arab world in search for a relation with its locality and history. The search for identity among Arab modern artists was tightly linked to regional political and cultural factors following the Second World War. With the decline of Western colonial power over the region, strong sentiments of nationalism and quests for cultural identity steered Arab countries and people. In an overview of modern Arab art, Wijdan Ali notes:

> It was this cultural reawakening which led to the third stage in the development of contemporary art in the Arab world. This search for national identity was preceded by several decades of stylistic homogeneity, during which Western tradition, rather than experimentation, was the guiding principle. . . . This cultural paradox induced them [the artists] to develop an indigenous art language based on traditional elements of Arabic art – including the arabesque, two-dimensional Islamic miniature painting, Arabic calligraphy, Eastern church icons, archaeological figures, ancient and modern legends, folk tales, Arabic literature and social and political events – but employing contemporary media and modes of interpretation.[7]

Such artistic explorations are particularly pronounced in the contributions of Arab modern artists to the posters centred on the Palestinian struggle (see fig. 1.1). This practice resonated in a number of the Lebanese war posters, in which local artists transposed their artwork from the canvas to the poster. An initial example is the artist Omran Kaysi (1943–) of Iraqi origin. Kaysi, who lived in Lebanon, was inspired by the Arabic calligraphy movement that emerged in Iraqi modern visual arts during the early 1970s and stimulated many other contemporary Arab artists. The formal language is premised on political consciousness of one's cultural position as well as spiritual groundings inspired by the aesthetic heritage of calligraphic gestures and the geometry of arabesque. Kaysi worked on posters during the early and mid-1980s that supported the national resistance against Israeli occupation, particularly centred on the solidarity with the southern coastal city of Saida (figs 1.2–1.5). Some of his posters took the form of abstract graphic explorations, featuring elaborate Arabic calligraphy and arabesque motifs adapted from the artist's own paintings and drawings.

In a different visual vocabulary, yet equally pertaining to local cultural heritage, the renowned Lebanese artist Rafic Charaf (1932–2003) also adapted his painting subjects into posters. He transposed mythical icons of Arab heroism from past times, found in old Arab poetry and folk tales, to a present moment of political struggle. His early political posters addressed the Arab struggle with Israel and praised the Palestinian resistance. By the mid-1980s, Charaf's posters were centred on the Lebanese national resistance in its fight to end Israeli occupation (fig. 1.6).

Paul Guiragossian (1926–93), another highly acclaimed Lebanese artist, had already been designing posters for some of the leading cultural events since the late 1960s. His poster contributions took a political turn during the war as he volunteered his artwork for the Lebanese Communist Party (LCP) and other civil organizations supporting the national resistance to Israeli occupation (figs 1.8–1.10). Guiragossian's poster compositions hold direct symbolism and resemble drawings in an artist's sketchbook. China ink and red wash paint dynamic human figures, silhouettes of anonymous heroes and workers in struggle for liberation.

Such examples of artist contributions in posters hold more the aesthetic qualities of a painting than those of a poster. The message is visually complex and highly interpretive, unlike a promotional poster designed to communicate swiftly and efficiently. Nevertheless, they reflect their authors' sense of belonging to a political struggle. Yet the authors' artistic practices continued to be their primary occupations, with occasional escapades from the canvas to the printed poster. This is often the case when the artist offers a painted portrait in tribute to an acclaimed political leader. Portraits in such posters reflected the artists' modern formal expression and sophisticated aesthetic representation. Such portrait-centred posters were unconventional with respect to the prevailing popular romantic realism or photographic portraiture of acclaimed leaders and election candidates.

This type of poster is exemplified by the abundant group centred on the commemoration of Kamal Jumblatt, founder of the Progressive Socialist Party and leader of the Lebanese National Movement, following his assassination in 1977. A number of renowned artists, namely Imad Abou Ajram (1940–), Wahib Bteddini (1929–), Jamil Molaeb (1948–), Aref el-Rayess (1928–2005) and Moussa Tiba (1939–), participated in paying tribute to the fallen leader (fig. 1.7). Resistance to Israeli occupation of South Lebanon has equally been the subject of many posters by prominent local artists. A number of these posters were issued by civil organizations, such as the Cultural Council for South Lebanon. The council grouped a number of Lebanese left-wing intellectuals and organized yearly cultural activities, exhibitions, conferences and publications, centred on the themes of national resistance and desires for liberation (figs 1.9–1.10).

Artists take on graphic design

Alternatively, a number of artists engaged in the poster design process as a total creative endeavour. In particular, those who in parallel to their artistic practice earned a professional experience in graphic design and illustration ultimately became familiar with the poster's functional requirements. They employed more simplified illustrations and planned graphic compositions, including photographic montages, which integrated the typographic/calligraphic message into the overall poster layout. While responding to modern currents of visual expression and the functional requirements of a poster, the artists did not fully share the aesthetic of an international design modernism that overwhelmed graphic design in the West during the 1960s. That movement, based on premises of functionalism and quests for a universal language of form, favoured a rational approach to graphic design over the subjective expression of the artist. At variance with Western approaches to modern design, the Arab artists brought to the poster their own distinctive artistic styles and cultural localities.

The concern for a culturally grounded and simplified pictorial approach is most common among the Palestinian posters, exemplified by the works of Burhan Karkutli (Syria, 1931–2000) and Helmi el-Touni (Egypt, 1934–). These, among a number of Arab artists, including Mohieddin Ellabbad (Egypt, 1940–), were part of an emerging collective in the early 1970s concerned with advancing illustrated Arabic books. Dar al-Fata al-Arabi, a publishing house specialized in Arabic children's books founded in 1974 in Beirut, acted as a pivotal point in modern illustrated Arabic books and a platform that grouped a number of creative talents in the Arab world. It offered a space to address contemporary issues of local social and political significance through popular means of graphic communication. A number of Dar al-Fata al-Arabi's publications were centred on the Palestinian cause and advocated the necessity of struggle to reclaim a lost homeland to a young readership.

Illustrations of such publications were often issued as posters. Among these are the works of Helmi el-Touni, who lived in Beirut from 1973 to 1983. As a politically engaged artist el-Touni was banned from practice in Egypt during Sadat's reign. He therefore moved to Beirut, where he worked as illustrator and designer for local publishing houses and cultural institutions. During his residency in Lebanon he designed posters for different political and civil rights organizations in addition to Lebanese left-wing and Arab nationalist parties. He particularly focused on the subject of popular resistance, where he always portrayed women as active social agents (figs 1.12, 1.28, 3.10 and 5.12). Helmi el-Touni has developed a formal language of his own inspired by the different visual manifestations of local popular culture from contemporary vernacular mural paintings in Egypt to indigenous North African tattoos, and the heritage of Islamic miniature painting. His illustrations are ripe with popular symbols and representations of hopeful imaginary realms, drawn in flattened compositions and simplified shapes defined by warm and bright colours.

The Syrian artist Youssef Abdelkeh (1951–), exiled from Syria, lived in Beirut for a short while before settling in Paris. Abdelkeh has equally engaged in children's book illustration with Dar al-Fata al-Arabi and poster design in parallel to his artwork. His main poster contributions, mostly to the Lebanese Communist Party to which he was affiliated, held straightforward graphic compositions while being aesthetically intriguing (fig. 1.13). The LCP, in fact, had the most varied poster contributions from prominent Lebanese artists: Samir Khaddage (1938–), Seta Manoukian (1954–), Emil Menhem (1951–) and Hussein Yaghi (1950–), in addition to the above-discussed posters of Guiragossian. These artists had already been involved in designing posters for Palestinian organizations and had formed among themselves a collaborative workspace. Among them, Emil Menhem has gained more interest in graphic design through his political poster experience and ultimately embraced the profession. Menhem also designed his own Arabic typefaces; he explains that his interest in Arabic type began while designing posters as he felt the need to create the appropriate modern Arabic type for each poster composition (fig. 1.14). Kameel Hawa is another similar case of an artist who shifted his career towards graphic design stimulated by his practice of designing political posters in the early phase of the war.[8] Hawa's political inclinations, on the other hand, were Arab nationalist, which brought him to design a significant number of posters for the Socialist Arab Union in Lebanon mostly centred on popular struggle. His posters vary between elaborate drawings and modern pictorial representations where his own Arabic hand lettering forms a dynamic integrated layer of the graphic composition (figs 1.15–1.16).

Networks of solidarity from Cuba to Beirut and back

The diverse posters discussed so far reveal the identifiable style and cultural specificity of the artist, responding to a general undercurrent of modern art in the Arab world. Nonetheless, a number of Arab political posters corresponded with the aesthetic genres of other contemporary anti-imperialist struggle and revolutionary movements' posters, particularly the solidarity posters issued by the Cuban-based OSPAAAL (Organization in Solidarity with the People of Africa, Asia, and Latin America). The poster compositions are essentially comparable in terms of the 1960s Pop aesthetics, pictorial abstraction and vigorous colours (figs 1.17–1.18).[9] In fact, the OSPAAAL posters were sent to Lebanon in coordination with the various Palestinian organizations and allied left-wing Lebanese parties. A number of the OSPAAAL posters were centred on the subjects of resistance and liberation in different Arab countries, among these the Palestinian resistance and Lebanon under Israeli occupation (figs 1.19–1.20). In a less abundant stream, the Palestinian organizations published a few posters in solidarity with revolutionary causes in Latin American countries. The Cuban artist Olivio Martinez narrates with emotive words this period's thrust of solidarity in political struggle:

> On many occasions, delegates of movements from three continents came and told me of their joy at the response to a specific poster among their particular fighting force and

nation, which adopted it as if it were their own. These times are among my greatest professional moments of happiness. . . . I'm referring to my 1972 poster for solidarity with the Palestinian people. This image was so heartfelt for them that they used it on the cover of an *Al Fateh* magazine . . . as their identifying logo for the movement's editorials in the publication. They admired it so much that on one of Yasser Arafat's visits to Cuba, Fidel presented him with the original artwork.[10]

Not only did the visual language of a number of Palestinian resistance posters respond to the Cuban graphics of the time, they are equally homologous in the iconographic representations pertaining to armed struggle, popular resistance and revolutionary discourse – heroic guerrilla, weapons (AK-47), clenched fist and depictions of imperial powers. This aesthetic, which was equally prevalent among the Lebanese posters, held the connotations of leftist politics of that era. In Lebanon, it meant not only Marxist politics but signified other forms of anti-imperialist and anti-Zionist struggles, which articulated revolutionary liberation struggles with Arab unionist quests. Arab nationalist parties therefore adopted this graphic language as much as parties with Marxist orientations (figs 1.21, 3.23, 4.26 and 5.19). The networks of aesthetic exchange were brought by the political alliances between Cuba and revolutionary movements in Arab countries. The Socialist Arab Union in Lebanon, for instance, sent student delegates from the party to a Youth Congress in Cuba held in 1981. The designer Kameel Hawa produced a multilingual poster for that occasion, highlighting Cuba's support and the relation of Abd-el-Nasser with both Che Guevara and Fidel Castro. The delegates from Lebanon also organized for that purpose an exhibition of posters in Cuba with the title *Exhibition of posters in support of the Palestinian revolution and the Arab identity of Lebanon* (figs 1.22–1.23).

Political cartoon and burlesque satire

Another aesthetic genre that typifies the political posters of the Lebanese civil war is characterized by the numerous contributions of political cartoonists to poster design. This typology of posters is probably the most evident. Political cartoon has figured in the Arab press since the early twentieth century. It has gained popularity over the years and established itself as a legitimate creative practice that combines artistic skills and wit with political expression, aimed towards a mass audience. It is unsurprising that such an aesthetic genre would be extended to political posters. These hold more direct political expression of the subject through a compositional arrangement heavy on symbolic signs. In turn, the signs are materialized by simplified figurative drawings relying on conventional political codes and literal visualizations of collective imaginings particular to the distinct communities being addressed. The drawings, marked by the signature style of the various authors, employ methods of exaggeration that highlight the political message and the subject's distinguishing features, ranging from heroic praise and glorification to burlesque caricature and political satire. While a number of local amateur cartoonists have been active on that front, I will exemplify my study of this poster genre with the works of two prominent Lebanese political cartoonists, Pierre Sadek and Nabil Kdouh, who produced a substantial number of posters during the war.

Pierre Sadek is a leading figure in political cartoon in Lebanon; he obtained numerous awards and international recognition for his political satire in the daily press. He published a book in 1977, comprising caricatures with overt commentary on the civil war politics, titled *Kulluna 'al watan* (*All [fighting] over the Nation*), a parody of the national anthem *Kulluna lil watan* ('All for the Nation'). Sadek, a vehement advocate of Lebanese nationalism, has volunteered his skills for numerous posters promoting the Lebanese army. He also contributed a considerable number of posters for the Lebanese Kataeb Party and its affiliated military organization, the Lebanese Forces (LF) (figs 2.15, 2.17, 3.4, 3.14 and 3.21). These were particularly abundant after the assassination in 1982 of Bashir Gemayel, military commander of the Lebanese Front and short-lived president of the Lebanese Republic, and centred on the commemoration of the lost leader. Sadek describes his political posters as a tribute to a leader he greatly admired, 'whose vision of Lebanon coincides with my own aspirations'.[11] In confirmation of his admiration and grief over the lost leader, he also published a drawing book in 1983 dedicated to the memory of Bashir Gemayel.

Besides posters, Pierre Sadek participated in other mass-media establishments of the LF during the 1980s. He illustrated covers for the magazine *al-Massira*, in addition to drawing daily caricatures for the television station LBC (Lebanese Broadcast Corporation). His signature style in political cartoons as well as illustrations is quickly discernable and can be traced in his poster work. Simplified forms and silhouetted shapes or portraits make up the central figures and symbols of his compositions. His black ink drawings are mostly rendered in vigorous cross-hatchings and hence create an intricate contrast between shaded areas and lit ones. The graphic elements are composed in a playful relation between positive and negative forms, designed against a flat minimalist background. These formal tactics added to the straightforwardness of the symbolic representations in his posters, create an eye-catching image that's hard to miss and require very little text to anchor the message, an approach typical to political cartoon.

Aside from Sadek, very few professionals contributed to the posters of the Lebanese Front parties. As the collection of political posters reveals and as confirmed by political officials in those parties, the production of posters within the Lebanese Front was relatively limited in comparison to the abundance of posters issued by their adversaries. That was due to several reasons that will be addressed towards the end of this chapter. Amateur illustrators drew the relatively few posters issued during the 1970s, which makes the political cartoon typology dominant among the Lebanese Front posters of that period, often with burlesque exaggeration and naive symbolism lacking the subtleties of Pierre Sadek (figs 5.13 and 5.15).

Nabil Kdouh is another professionally trained political cartoonist who executed a substantial number of posters during the civil war period. He, on the other hand, contributed mostly to factions within the Lebanese National Movement. His political cartoon for the LNM newspaper *al-Watan* has prompted various parties of the LNM – the Progressive Socialist Party, the Syrian Social Nationalist Party and the Independent Nasserist Movement (Murabitun) – to solicit his illustrations for their magazine covers as well as their posters. Kdouh claims he had no political engagement, nor adherence to any party; this allowed him to take commissions from parties with diverging ideological frameworks. Illustration became his profession, he says. Nevertheless, being originally from the south of Lebanon, he became more inclined in the 1980s to work on illustrations representing national belonging and popular resistance to occupation. Since then, Nabil Kdouh mostly designed posters for the Amal movement, while still maintaining that he never adhered to the party's political activities. His affiliation, as he explains, was based on shared belonging and his admiration for the movement's leader.[12]

Kdouh closely collaborated with Amal's media office to devise each poster's message; the media director would develop the text, which in turn would inspire Kdouh to illustrate. Relying on freehand ink drawing and aquarelle tints, his illustrations are rich with details, resulting in posters that appear like visually recounted narratives resembling popular comics. The purpose, according to Kdouh, is to convey the poster message through direct visual representations, which can be easily accessible to a large audience comprising rural areas that hold a high rate of illiteracy (figs 2.13, 3.22, 4.28, 5.10 and 5.11). Through his poster drawings, Nabil Kdouh has moved from satire to expressive illustrations. He eventually got more inclined to children's illustrations, which became his profession, and withdrew entirely from political posters towards the end of the war.

Popular realism and politico-religious imaginings

As icons of political leadership gained more intensity during the civil war, leaders' portraits pervaded the public space. Aside from posters, immense painted portraits governed over symbolic locations within communities' territorial claims. The phenomenon was amplified in the 1980s, as the country witnessed further segregation according to tight sectarian divides and battles over territories. Specialized promotional hoardings painters were solicited to execute the mega-scale portraits of political figures. Muhammad Moussalli, a self-trained painter who began his career in the 1960s mainly doing portraits of electoral candidates and advertisements for multinational commercial brands, had during the war a long waiting list of commissions from various political factions (figs 1.24–1.25). Moussalli recounts how he was esteemed by his 'high-positioned clients' and was often called 'the king of portraiture'.[13] He explains that the artistry lay not only in getting the portrait as close as possible to reality but in rendering the figure charismatic and more appealing than reality. Moussalli would produce a series of up to 70–100 similar hand-painted portraits for the same political figure during the war period, so as to fulfil manually the function of a mechanically mass-produced poster.[14]

Additionally, painters of Arab film hoardings designed political posters in the same romanticized style normally assigned for the promotion of films. One example is Mahmoud Zeineddine; he extended his painting skills to printed posters, chiefly for the Progressive Socialist Party to which he ascribed his Druze belonging. The aesthetics of popular realism and romanticism associated with the promotion of films and star actors was transposed, in Zeineddine's posters, to portraits of mythical leaders and scenes of military heroism (fig. 1.26).

The romanticized version of realist painting was prevalent amongst the emerging Islamic movements of the mid-1980s. It is particularly abundant in posters honouring the fallen martyrs of the Islamic Resistance, the military wing of Hizbullah. Throughout the 1980s Hizbullah's media office would have a portrait painted in oils for each martyr, which would be offered to the martyr's family and ultimately used for the poster. The compositions featured idyllic portraits of the deceased and narratives surrounding the religious sanctity in which the struggle and martyrdom were inscribed (see chapter 4). The posters present pseudo-realist painted compositions of imaginative settings derived from a repertoire of religious representations in Shi'ite history and mythology. That kind of aesthetics offers the possibility to render what is collectively imagined, in terms of religious texts and symbols, into realist yet simultaneously mythical images with popular appeal (fig. 1.27).

The case of Hizbullah's media office presents an exception to the prevailing models of poster production by political parties discussed above. After informally relying on networks of affiliated artists and resources, by 1985 Hizbullah had a full-fledged set-up for artistic production within its media structure. The party provided a collective workspace, equipped with the needed tools and resources, including a library of references on political art and posters. The work process on the posters was mostly collaborative, involving the different skills of experts engaged in the workshop team. An illustrator/designer handled the conception of the poster and acted as the art director, a painter worked on the portraits, a calligrapher attended to the titling and Koranic inscriptions and a technician handled the preparation for printing. The painters and calligraphers were also involved in other media projects besides posters, such as mural paintings, public hoardings and banners – *yafta*. The specialized members were mostly adherents to the party; they shared its ideology and religious convictions and hence operated from within the party's discourse. This facilitated an autonomous process of communication and message encoding of the posters by the team members without the dictation of the political bureau, as one member of the design team describes. Muhammad Ismail joined Hizbullah's media office in 1984 and became a leading designer at the workshop until 1994.[15] Ismail studied Fine Arts at the Lebanese University and practised illustration and political cartoon while he held a job at a printing press before he joined the office and helped in establishing it. His artistic inclination and skills in drawing in addition to his knowledge of printing, as he explains, aided him in the graphic design process.

Hizbullah's posters in the beginning were based on a compounding of previous experiences in political posters: Socialist realism, the Palestinian resistance and the Iranian Revolution posters. As a resistance movement against Israeli occupation, Hizbullah shared with these the iconography of subversion of imperialist powers and armed struggle for national liberation. Hizbullah's members had in fact been previously engaged with leftist resistance movements, Palestinian and Lebanese parties, and in most part belonged to the Shi'ite-based Amal movement. The Iranian poster model was most useful since it imbued the anti-imperialist struggle with a politico-religious discourse that is pertinent to Hizbullah and familiar to its Shi'ite community. The Shi'ite community particularly originating from South Lebanon and the Bekaa valley, which makes up Hizbullah's adherents, in fact shared with Iran a history of cultural and religious practices and symbolic representations pertaining to Shi'ism.

As will be discussed in the following chapters, the shared Shi'ite politico-religious discourse, institutionalized through the building of the Islamic Republic of Iran,[16] facilitated transposing the iconography and aesthetics of Iranian posters and adapting them into the Lebanese context. The Islamic Republic, in its pan-Islamic Shi'ite framework, has provided Hizbullah with religious and political guidance through the party's pledged allegiance to *Wilayat al-Faqih* (the guardianship of the jurisprudent) under the leadership of Khomeini and his successor Khamini'i.[17] Concurrently, Iran has supplied the party with resources and support that enabled the establishment and continued institutional development of the political party and its paramilitary resistance to the Israeli occupation of South Lebanon. Among these resources were also Iranian methods of modern political art. The members of the media office at Hizbullah received training in artistic skills and poster design from Iranian artists who came to Lebanon for short workshops in the early period of the party's establishment. During their short residency in Lebanon, these Iranian artists designed some of the early posters produced between 1983 and 1985, including Hizbullah's logo, which is based on that of the Iranian Revolutionary Guards (Pasderan).

Likewise, some of Hizbullah's early posters make use not only of the iconography and aesthetic genre but also of the same drawings present in Iranian posters. A recurrent example is the colourful illustration of the religious shrine and pan-Islamic symbol of Jerusalem the Dome of the Rock (figs 1.28–1.31; see chapter 3). In fact the symbol had been fairly well known to a Lebanese audience familiar with the Palestinian liberation movement. Chelkowski and Dabashi, in their book *Staging a Revolution: The Art of Persuasion in the Islamic Republic of Iran*, claim that the Iranian artists had originally been influenced by Palestinian iconography on this matter through an exhibition of Palestinian political art, brought from Beirut and held in Tehran in 1979.[18] This particular colourful drawing of the Dome of the Rock had in fact been originally painted by the Egyptian illustrator Helmi el-Touni. It features on a poster issued in the 1970s by the Beirut-based publishing house Dar al-Fata al-Arabi. The icon of the Dome of the Rock had thus made quite a journey before it found itself back on the streets of Beirut in the mid-1980s through Hizbullah's posters.

Beyond the particularities of the overtly religious rhetoric of Hizbullah's posters, their aesthetic vocabulary does not constitute a unified typology that can be distinguished from other aesthetic practices of political posters of the Lebanese civil war. Besides the religiously inscribed romanticized painting, Hizbullah's posters often resorted to modern means of design – abstract graphic representations, and montage of photography with illustration – evident in the work of Muhammad Ismail. The eclectic character of Hizbullah's posters corresponds to the articulated structure of their politico-religious discourse as an Islamic Resistance in Lebanon. It is also analogous to the hybrid aesthetics of the Iranian experience, which articulated codes of revolutionary struggle with religious signs of Shi'ite collective imaginary (fig. 1.32).

Concluding remarks

As the war persisted over 16 years, internal hostilities were aggravated. The decline of basic premises of humanity, rise to power of warlords and militia hegemony, combined with the economic breakdown of the country and the emotional loss that the Lebanese have suffered, ultimately reflected back on the quality of posters. Needless to say, the parties' growing military pursuits throughout the war evidently lowered their attention to the aesthetic quality of posters. Posters became a symbolic means to assert a party's military hegemony over an area; for that purpose, the party's logo and leader's portrait sufficed to symbolically mark the claimed territories.

Artists mostly on the left side of the local politics, who were taken by the fervour of progressive projects and revolutionary causes of the 1960s and 70s, withdrew from their activism as the struggle diverged from its initial reformist goals and crept along narrow confessional lines and into irrational violence. The networks of artistic collaboration that were instated by the alliance of Lebanese parties with Palestinian organizations were severed by the Israeli invasion and the subsequent withdrawal of the PLO from Beirut in 1982. With the exception of efforts put into posters supporting the national resistance to Israeli occupation during the 1980s, the utopian fervour of the previous decades was followed by a decreased interest in political participation and a general sense of distrust. It left the majority of poster design in the hands of media officials, who kept on reproducing the same template formats for most of the posters issued by the party.

On the other hand the opposing camp, the Lebanese Front, had, to begin with, very few contributions from professionals. Compared to their adversaries, the parties that formed the Lebanese Front produced relatively very few posters. Besides Pierre Sadek's engagement with the Kataeb party and the Lebanese Forces, there were hardly any other prominent artists or professionals contributing to their poster production. There are many reasons to explain this. First of all, as I have already addressed, the artists' abundant poster contributions on the left had begun before the war with the Palestinian resistance and coincided with a movement of political engagement among Arab artists with current regional political struggles. These surpassed the specificity of Lebanon and encompassed the Arab–Israeli conflict as well as progressive socio-political struggles. Such sentiments were not shared among the adherents to the Lebanese Front. In fact they were contested by strong affirmations of Lebanese nationalism, as opposed to an Arab one, in addition to right-wing conservatism pronounced by the parties forming the Lebanese Front. Thus the poster practice as a form of artistic political engagement and tool for struggle was a phenomenon particularly tied to left-wing politics and historically linked with revolutionary ideals, from the Bolshevik poster to the Cuban solidarity posters and contemporaneous protest movements.

A second reason is that the Palestinian organizations, based on their own rich experience in the production of posters and through their alliance with the left-wing parties, provided the latter with a creative framework in which the design of political posters could flourish. They equally supplied their allied Lebanese parties with the needed material and human resources for the production of posters.

A third reason is more speculative. It relates to the geopolitics of the war and the nature of the poster as medium of dissemination within the public space. The media offices of the various parties held networks of poster distribution within their own areas of political control. The posters in that sense also acted as a symbolic affirmation of a party's hegemony over a certain territory. The western sector of Beirut was shared as a territorial space among many political parties, which formed, in the 1970s through the early 1980s, the combined forces of the Palestinian organizations and the Lebanese National Movement. It eventually witnessed, in the mid-1980s, the rise of the Islamic Resistance amidst other secular parties which formed the National Resistance Front against Israeli occupation. Aside from rural areas, whose territories were clearly demarcated, west Beirut was a contested terrain of multiple hegemonic articulations by the various parties that fought to maintain their territorial control. This had resulted in multiplied efforts in the production of posters among the different parties supposedly belonging to the same camp. In consequence, central locations in west Beirut witnessed a sort of symbolic competition of politically diverse posters. Media officials recount how posters they put on walls would often be covered the next day by other posters from a different party.

Such a symbolic battle and race in poster production was not practised in the eastern sector of Beirut. To start with, the Lebanese Front included fewer parties than the opposing camp. Additionally, from 1976 the small military groupings dismembered to join the Lebanese Forces commanded by Bashir Gemayel, who by 1980 unified all contingent parties of the front under his command. The unchallenged hegemony of the Lebanese Forces over the Christian eastern sector of Beirut did not lead to the competition and heavy production of posters among parties that west Beirut experienced. In the mid-80s, the Lebanese Forces invested in television broadcast and periodical publication as overreaching mass media and declined their poster activities. The later political discords and battles in the so-called 'Christian territories' between 1989 and 1990 were pronounced instead through these mass media.

PART II

Themes, Icons and Signs

2

Leadership

Whether in the service of democracy or dictatorship, during the twentieth century artists and graphic designers have been responsible for the lion's share of hero mongering. They have painted the paintings, drawn the drawings, and designed the icons that impress a leader's likeness on mass consciousness.[1]

From Fascist 'demigod' to revolutionary 'heroic guerrilla', the cult of the heroic leader has travelled across continents and been employed by the various movements that shaped twentieth-century politics. Stalin, Mussolini, Hitler, Mao Zedong, Che Guevara and many others have had their image reproduced on massive quantities of posters. The poster image, through a creative mix of iconic and symbolic signs, renders the mythical qualities attributed to the leader readily visible and almost factual. The leader appears through the image to be 'naturally' endowed with those heroic qualities. Writing on the deification of Mussolini, Simonetta Falasca-Zamponi notes: 'The image of Mussolini as omnipresent, valiant and heroic invested the Duce with a magical, mystical aura that placed him above common people – or, better, above mortals.'[2] In an altogether different political framework but similar process, the popular icon of Che Guevara, the subject of closely similar graphic adaptations of the same photograph taken by Alberto Korda in 1960, has fixed meanings of revolutionary zeal onto the young man's face. Rick Poynor notes that after Che's charismatic image has been overused and commodified, it still retains today its symbolic power.[3]

In their iconography, the signifiers of leadership share an age-old, global format for representing the heroic or mythical figure of the official leader – the portrait. The proliferation of a modern typology of heroic portraiture in twentieth-century political posters is largely influenced by an older practice of idealized representations of Greek and Roman emperors as well as official portraiture of Western nobility and royalty. The tools of reproduction and graphic lexicons may change with the place and era, yet certain stereotypes persist.[4] This is not to say that all leadership portraiture looks alike: heroic personas vary according to the needs of the cultural and political climate in which these figures emerge, and consequently new forms come to embody the distinct leaders.

Strong allegiance to personality cults is clearly visible in the dominance of the leadership theme among the sample of posters produced in wartime Lebanon. More than one-third of the poster collection is dedicated solely to the veneration of leaders, besides other posters that serve different purposes yet incorporate a reference to a leader, portrait or quotation. As many factions and political communities strove for power on the Lebanese war scene, a number of leaders emerged as the custodians of their own communities. A short look inside the peculiar phenomenon of political leadership in Lebanon deserves our attention before I move into a reading of leadership iconography in Lebanon's political posters.

Lebanon's *za'im* phenomenon

> Middle Eastern politics are highly personalized. To Westerners, personality cults in Arab states, parties and militias are indistinguishable from iconography or hagiography. Portraits and photographs rather than uniforms and flags show which group controls which area. Political allegiance attaches primarily to persons, and only secondarily to organizations and programs.[5]

Leadership, or *za'ama*, is a very particular and recurrent phenomenon in the political and social structure of Lebanon. Different parties and political communities offer strong allegiance to the leader figure, *za'im*, and they have a tendency to glorify their leaders – especially their party founders – to the point that they are often criticized for being the parties of leaders rather than of sustainable programmes. The *za'im* phenomenon precedes the war period; it is deeply rooted in the socio-political history of pre-independent Lebanon.[6] Arnold Hottinger, writing in 1966, defines the *za'im* in Lebanon as 'the political leader who possesses the support of a locally circumscribed community and who retains this support by fostering or appearing to foster the interests of as many as possible from amongst his clientele'.[7] He traces the patterns of *za'ama* historically from feudal tutelage to administrative office and governmental functions institutionalized under the Ottoman rule and French mandate over Lebanon. He also examines how post-Second World War economic and political transformations have engendered two new varieties of *zu'ama* (leaders): the prosperous businessman and the political activist, ideological spokesman of a community. Hottinger distinguishes modern organized parties from the more traditional *za'im* patronage, opening the question at the end of his essay on the prospect of modern party democracy in Lebanon ruling out the 'antiquated system'.

Samir Khalaf argues, in his essay 'Changing forms of political patronage', that the forms of patronage have changed; yet the traditional basis of authority attributed to the *za'im* figure has been socially sustained by kinship loyalty and legitimized by the political system through the electoral process. 'Like confessionalism,' Khalaf claims, 'patronage has become almost institutionalized into Lebanon's body politic.'[8] The position of leadership is largely maintained within traditional political families, frequently passed on from father to son. The perpetuation of political power through hereditary succession, as in nobilities, has persisted through the different forms of patronage mentioned above and been applied within the 'more modern institutions' such as political parties and parliamentary elections.[9]

With the advent of the war, party democracy gave way to intense armed conflict and to a heightened sectarian consciousness; the *za'im* figure got amplified into a mythical hero, protector of his community and its sectarian interest. Farid el-Khazen notes with regards to the Maronite community: 'In times of crisis, "strong men" are needed. They become the de facto spokesmen of their communities. As conflict intensifies, these leaders come to embody the qualities of heroism ingrained in communal mythology: physical daring, defiance of authority, the self-inflated importance of the community, and the unwavering willingness to resist and even to die for the cause.'[10]

A leader was commemorated – particularly after his assassination – as the heroic figure and role model that a given party relied on to lend its struggle credibility and continuity. A quotation from the leader is sometimes used to emphasize certain beliefs that must not be forgotten and so are perpetuated in the public realm. These quotations have been repeated on different posters throughout the years. In other instances, specific quotations resurface, to be rewritten into the changing political moment as the war unfolds. In most cases, the name is never mentioned next to the portrait. It doesn't need to be, as one can safely assume that the audience is contemporaneous and familiar with the figure. (However, that is not the case when the leader is commemorated a long time after his death.) The portrait, it seems, acts as a visual code referring directly to the leader figure, replacing the linguistic one (name), acquired among other codes and stored in the collective memory of the community. On many posters, portraits of leaders mystically float above figures of active combatants, in an attempt to boost their morale at critical moments of the fighting and to 'bless' their battles, suggesting that the leader is present 'in spirit' among them and assists them in their hardship and victory. Leaders, their speech immortalized, enter the realm of myth, fixed by their portrait's reference to a frozen ideological moment. The city, the street, and the partisans fall under their watchful gaze.

In the following sections, I will discuss the diverse iconography reserved for three highly popular wartime Lebanese leaders who have had considerable representation in political posters: Kamal Jumblatt (1917–77), Bashir Gemayel (1947–82), and Mussa al-Sadr (1928–disappeared in 1978). While each led a major political faction and ideological current during the war, these leaders also came to represent, throughout the war, narrow and distinct confessional communities: Druze, Maronite and Shi'ite. Absent from these are posters of Sunni leadership. Political movements that have gathered mainly Sunni followers are mostly Nasserist in orientation; in most of their posters, Gamal Abd-el-Nasser features as the quintessential *za'im*. On the other hand, Antun Saadeh, the Syrian Social Nationalist Party founder, who was executed in 1949, continued to be the quintessential *za'im* figure on the party's posters during the war, as will be discussed in chapter 3. His posters will not be part of our analysis here, since this chapter is mainly concerned with the wartime leaders.

As for the Lebanese Communist Party and the Organization of Communist Action, which played major roles in the war and produced a serious number of political posters, I did not come across any poster representation of leadership, be it local or international. This seem to be uncommon, since most Communist parties worldwide have produced icons of mythical heroes, from Soviet Russia's portraits of Lenin and Stalin, China's larger-than-life portraits of Mao, to Cuba's icon of Che Guevara and the many leftist resistance movements across the world that have followed suit. Many reasons might be inferred from this. One, that the icon of the left was reserved to Kamal Jumblatt as leader of the Lebanese National Movement. Second, that the Communist parties' critical and reformist stance vis-à-vis traditional *za'ama* in Lebanon held them back from entering that iconographic discourse. Third, that the parties' secular stance and multi-confessional base is not the typical environment in which a Lebanese *za'im* in the parochial terms addressed earlier could flourish.

Kamal Jumblatt – the ascetic socialist

Is there anything more noble than crossing over the bridge of death into the life that revives others and genuinely supports their cause and that strengthens the model of resistance and sacrifice in the souls of activists?

Kamal Jumblatt

This quotation from Kamal Jumblatt before his assassination on 16 March 1977 occupies the dark side of a poster while the other side depicts Jumblatt crossing into a peaceful blue sky (fig. 2.1). These poetic words, used on a number of posters, were probably meant to honour those who had died in their struggle. For Jumblatt's admirers these words were premonitory of his heroic fate: the role model for martyrdom, genuine resistance and sacrifice. The assassination of Kamal Jumblatt, founder and leader of the Progressive Socialist Party and the head of the Lebanese National Movement, is by far the most commemorated subject in the political posters of the Lebanese war and accordingly he is the leader most represented in posters. Above 100 posters of Kamal Jumblatt were produced by the PSP, LNM and PLO; these amount to half the total number of posters available on leadership.

Following the assassination of Kamal Jumblatt, 1 May (International Labour Day) was declared Jumblatt's international day in 1977. By being commemorated on this specific day, Jumblatt is closely tied with an occasion of international significance for all leftist movements, beyond the Progressive Socialist Party membership and that of the Lebanese left, as is clear from the use of multiple languages on a poster produced for that effect (fig. 2.2). A modern graphic illustration equally praises the Arab and international magnitude of Jumblatt: his portrait, a three-quarter face with a slight upward tilt, resides on top of a map of the Arab world. The world globe behind him, he gazes nobly at an undefined realm ahead. The illustration was used as a logo for numerous posters and publications that were produced for commemorations of this day. The image was reproduced for the first and second annual commemorations of his assassination with minor alterations, a frank frontal pose in black and white instead of the three-quarter one (fig. 2.3). In a poster designed for the occasion of 1 May 1977, Jumblatt figures again as an international hero among the legendary leaders of resistance and liberation movements of world history: Gamal Abd-el-Nasser (Egypt), Patrice Lumumba (Congo), Che Guevara (Cuba), Ho Chi Minh (Vietnam), and Tanios Chahine (leader of a peasant revolt in nineteenth-century Lebanon), who have fought a common cause 'Against imperialism and Zionism', as is stated by the poster's title. The flashy colours and graphic rendering of the portraits aesthetically reference the 1960s and 70s OSPAAAL solidarity posters produced in Cuba; the poster is very much embedded within the graphic style of left-wing anti-imperialist posters of the time (fig. 1.21).

Against the stereotype icon of a reckless revolutionary hero of the radical left, Jumblatt's portrait appears to be gentle, humble and in fact very peaceful. These traits hardly coincide with the chauvinist Lebanese *za'im* equation addressed earlier, the 'strong men' who are physically daring and defiant. Yet he was undoubtedly 'the *za'im*' of Lebanon's left, 'the symbol for a democratic and secular Arab Lebanon', who called for 'a unified national movement and a victorious Palestinian resistance' and who 'gave his life for the Palestinian cause and a united Arab destiny', as clearly affirmed on the many posters that exalted his leadership through textual messages (figs 2.8–2.11). These posters, mostly produced by the LNM media office, relied on text as the main message, set in a standardized calligraphic composition; the text alternates between an Arab rhetoric of praise and highly charged quotations by Jumblatt.

While portraits of idealized leaders rely on embellishment, exaggerating the traits of the subject so that his 'body natural' coincides with the leader's 'body politic', at first sight Kamal Jumblatt's portrait appears awkwardly natural. Have the artists forgotten the trick of their trade? It is only after repeated exposure to his portraits on the different posters that one realizes that an icon has been produced: deep wrinkles on his forehead, raised eyebrows, a contemplative gaze, and a silent pensive expression (figs 2.2 and 2.4–2.5). This is surely not a portrait innocent of artifice; it is replete with signs synonymous with his peculiar political persona. Kamal Jumblatt was known by his admirers as a 'deep intellectual', a 'serious and sincere politician', a 'wise man who struggled patiently for the cause of justice', a 'vehement socialist' who received the Lenin prize, a humble man despite being a Jumblatti – descendant of a powerful Druze feudal family – and simultaneously as a spiritual man who practised daily meditation.[11] Farid el-Khazen's words on Jumblatt articulate the paradox in the leader's iconography:

> His mysterious ascetic-like charisma and negligent physical appearance – unusual among Lebanon's *zu'amah* – invited pity rather than admiration, and no other Arab leader was able to inspire pity while commanding so much power. In a masculine culture where physical appearance is generally a prerequisite for political culture, the guru-like Jumblatt was a striking exception to the rule.[12]

In a country where so much importance is attributed to the founder and leader of a political party, the death of a figure such as Kamal Jumblatt may be detrimental to the continuance of the party, let alone a whole movement. So signs of leadership, in text and image, are not depicted on posters solely for the purpose of glorification. They are in fact used as tools to ensure continuity of purpose in the minds and hearts of partisans: the heroic model and the emotional bond need to be sustained especially under the dire circumstances of warfare.

Representations of Jumblatt, after his death, as the spiritual guardian of his party's continuity in struggle and perseverance on the battlefront are many. His portrait, in a complacent facial expression, hovers over a crowd of people unified in armed struggle: 'He will remain with us and we shall reach victory' asserts the title of a poster. Another poster depicts, in an allegorical illustration, a powerful grip firmly surging upwards out of a fiery blast and waving the PSP flag that simultaneously materializes into Jumblatt's portrait. Concurrently, the poster depicts combatants in the heat of battle confirming their 'pledge and loyalty' to their leader in the eighth annual commemoration of his assassination (fig. 2.12).

Continuity of an altogether different sort is the subject of a poster showing Kamal Jumblatt with his son (fig. 2.13). Kamal Jumblatt's son, Walid, succeeded him not only as the leader of the PSP but also as the head of the LNM. After all, Kamal Jumblatt's early entry into politics had been based on an inherited title of Druze leadership as a member of the Jumblatt family; he was elected into parliament before establishing the Progressive Socialist Party. In the poster, Walid Jumblatt sits confidently while behind him stands a ghostly rendering of his father; larger than life he watches over. The poster's title, 'A pledge is a pledge', is a phrase often repeated by Jumblatt the son after he took office; the new za'im exemplifies here the role model for 'loyalty', loyalty to the role model set before him.

During the 1980s in Lebanon, as inter-confessional battles multiplied over territorial rule and sectarian consciousness tightened, Kamal Jumblatt 'the symbol of progressive and secular Arab Lebanon' gave way to a traditional Druze za'im in the representations of the PSP. A poster dating to 1984 displays Jumblatt's portrait along with the Druze religious flag and in the company of combatants in traditional mountain attire symbolic of machismo and heroism (fig. 2.14). The progressive project of an unconventional leader did not conform to the political reality of the 1980s in Lebanon. A change of image and reconstitution of the past into a present reality seemed necessary; the pledged 'loyalty' seems to ascribe to narrow confessional lines more than grand political projects.

Bashir Gemayel – the youthful militant

> Partout collée sur les murs, les portes, les poteaux, les voitures, à des milliers d'exemplaires, la photographie de Béchir Gemayel candidat à la présidence de la République, ne portait qu'un mot: 'L'Espoir'. Le lendemain de sa mort, un journal français titrait: «L'Espoir assassiné».[13]

Assassinated at the age of 34, Bashir Gemayel entered the collective consciousness and hearts of many Lebanese, particularly Christians, as a national hero and the youngest martyr president. He was the leader of the Lebanese Forces and son of the Kataeb founder and leader Pierre Gemayel. Thus he represented the 'ultimate hope for the salvation of Lebanon'. Many memorized his famous statement 'We will not give up one metre of the 10,452 km² that constitute our national territory.' '10,452 km²' became an expression magically linked to the 'hope' Bashir Gemayel had brought among his community. That 'mad hope', hailed as such by his people, was assassinated when at its peak, on 14 September 1982, only 22 days after Bashir Gemayel's election as president of the Lebanese Republic (23 August), leaving his admirers in utter disbelief at his sudden disappearance, and in a communal state of disarray and depression.[14]

Posters displayed to celebrate his victory in the presidential elections had still been up when others were posted to mourn his death. The posters initially intended to disseminate joy conveyed an opposite meaning after 14 September. A photograph of Gemayel showed him held on the shoulders of young men exalting in their hero. It was later retouched to highlight only the winning president and the praising hands of followers around him. Diffused in the form of a large-scale poster, the photograph inscribed that moment in Lebanese history; reproduced almost yearly, the poster is still visible today in the streets of Ashrafieh, in the eastern sector of Beirut (fig. 2.16).

Besides the famous photographic one, a great number of posters were designed to mourn the young leader's absence on the two famous dates – 23 August and 14 September. These helped construct the narrative of the legendary hero of 'hope' in the collective consciousness of the Christian community. In one poster, Bashir Gemayel's portrait is suspended above the ground in a celestial dark blue setting. His profile is a paradoxical representation of both his presence and absence: the empty white silhouette, like a footprint on sand, tells us that he is no longer here, yet the 'national hero' adorned by a Lebanese flag has left a big mark in 'our' sky. The white profile is immediately recognized as that of Bashir when coupled with '23 August'. It is in fact based on the profile in the popular photograph mentioned above. The ribbonlike Lebanese flag stretches out of the LF logo, like a film reel unfolding the narrative of a national icon, extending endlessly into the perspective of the celestial blue (fig. 2.17). In a similar blue setting, another poster commemorates the date of his assassination: this time his photographic portrait is enclosed in a disc from which emanates a white saintly halo. The whole iconography borrows from representations of divine Christian figures; a diffused sun shines through the clouds and touches the 'blessed' with its divine light. From here, the rays proceed to shine on the map of Lebanon, on all the '10,452 km² that constitute our national territories' (fig. 2.18).

In 1976 Bashir Gemayel took charge of the Lebanese Forces, the unified military command of the Christian militias; by 1980 it became the only commanding Christian military power in Lebanon. The political groups that had once operated within the Lebanese Front were forcefully dissolved and absorbed into the organized structure of the Lebanese Forces, under the continued command of Gemayel. With that, he came to represent a new generation of politico-military leaders: he became the idol of a young and radicalized generation of Christians, dissatisfied with the accommodating rhetoric of traditional leaders. Samir Khalaf describes Bashir as follows: 'He had all the ingredients of an inspiring charismatic leader: youthful, engaging, highly energetic and spirited, firm in his convictions, and clear-sighted in his visions about Lebanon's future. Even his demeanour was refreshingly different: casual in appearance, personable and modest, he articulated his views in candid, simple, and colloquial Arabic.'[15]

The loss of a president was one thing; the loss of an idolized military leader necessitates another type of posters. A communal state of apathy and depression had taken hold of the LF combatants after the loss of their idol in 1982. It needed a whole mediatic process to convince them that their leader would not have approved of their submissive reaction when 'their' Lebanon was still under threat. A poster fashioned on the famous US 'I want you' recruitment poster campaign[16] replaced Uncle Sam, an imaginary American hero figure, with a powerful portrait of Bashir Gemayel. With the LF flag behind him, his finger pointing, his gaze fixed, the angry Bashir hails the combatants: 'Our Lebanon needs you, YOU.' The clouds beneath his portrait suggest that he speaks to them from the other side of life, from the position of the martyred hero whose place is among the angels. The poster creates a powerful interpolation that is difficult to avoid. In wartime, with the absence of consensus on the political identity of Lebanon, 'Our Lebanon' can be read as in 'different from theirs' but also as in 'rightfully ours', a Lebanon that 'we', Bashir speaking to a Christian community, 'should not abandon' (fig. 2.15).

Around 1983, many such posters were produced and other media efforts put in place to boost the morale of the young combatants, building on their memory and passion for their lost idol, in order to mobilize them to pursue 'the journey Bashir Gemayel had heroically started'.[17] The time coincides with the fierce battles that took hold in the mountains in 1983–4 between the LF and the PSP, resulting in major losses among the LF and a massive displacement of Christian communities from their home villages. '. . . Continuing the procession' is the title of another poster that aims at recruiting and mobilizing young combatants (fig. 3.14), published on 13 April 1983 in commemoration of the beginning of the civil war (see chapter 3).

Such representations, and there were many, helped to construct an exemplary icon of the heroic combatant and to consolidate the myth of Bashir Gemayel.[18] His portrait was omnipresent. Posters occupied the streets, schools, universities and homes of Lebanon's Christian regions. Like a pop star, his posters equally adorned the rooms of infatuated adolescents and local neighbourhood shops.[19] LF politicians began to close their public speeches with the statement *Bashir hayy fina liyabqa Lubnan* ('Bashir lives in us so that Lebanon remains'). It soon became a vehement slogan reiterated by the young combatants, determined to continue his journey.

Mussa al-Sadr – the turbaned activist

Mussa al-Sadr, a Shi'ite cleric of Iranian origin who acquired the title of Imam, was a reformer and an activist particularly attentive to the immense social needs of the Shi'ite community residing mainly in the largely undeveloped and deprived areas of South Lebanon, the Bekaa region and Beirut suburbs, neglected for a long time by the Lebanese state. He realized a number of projects and institutions providing educational, social and religious services to his community, in an attempt to fill the gap that the state and traditional Shia *zu'ama* had left unattended. Mussa al-Sadr established, in 1974, the Movement of the Disinherited, voicing the demands of the under-privileged Shi'ite community and arguably of the Lebanese deprived classes: 'It is the movement of all the disinherited . . . of those who feel deprivation in their actuality, of those who feel anxious for their future, and of those who shoulder their responsibility toward the disinherited and the anxious with honour and enthusiasm. It is the Lebanese movement for the best.'[20]

He was committed to the demands of his community while also seeking intercommunal dialogue and insisting that Lebanon's experiment of multi-confessionalism must succeed.[21] In a symbolic act that marked the consciousness of many Lebanese, the Imam delivered a captivating public speech at a Catholic cathedral in Beirut just a few months before violence got hold of the city; the violence at which he would later protest and lead a hunger strike in June 1975. In August 1978, Mussa al-Sadr mysteriously disappeared while on a visit to Libya. The words of Ghassan Tueni, writer and publisher of the local newspaper *An-Nahar*, capture with eloquence the politico-religious leader's mystique:

> Calm, 'the tranquil force', his face marked with deep gentleness, the Imam Mussa al-Sadr seemed to come from nowhere . . . By his charisma, he obliged his enemies and friends alike to venerate him, to respect his clairvoyance . . . [He was] tall, very tall: To the point of seeming to soar above the often frenzied crowds that his presence drew together: black turban tilted with a slight negligence. His enemies seemed charmed by his enigmatic and benevolent smile, whereas his friends found that his bearded face constantly reflected melancholy . . . One often had the impression that his immense head was constantly trying to rise even higher. And his hands gave the impression of gathering up his floating robe, the *abaya* in which he wrapped himself, as if he were preparing himself to step out of some antique miniature.

Even while he harangued the masses, his words were calm and sibylline, an oracle of love and hope, punctuated with mysterious accents of some mystic vision that appealed as much to reason as to the heart.

His personal contacts were a ritual of seduction. When he would humbly open the door and invite you to enter a modest office or an ordinary salon of some home which sheltered him, one would wonder why this man was there, by what mystery, and how such a mythic persona could seem so familiar. Then, as in a Persian miniature, one would sit at his feet, looking to reap the teachings of the master, only to leave with more questions than one had brought him.[22]

Mussa al-Sadr's poster-portrait, a familiar yet enigmatic icon, continues to cast the Imam's gentle gaze onto the inhabitants of many Shia neighbourhoods in Lebanon today (fig. 2.19). The two portrait representations, the written one above and the other in image form, are in magical accord with one another, as if the artist who drew the portrait made sure to incarcerate all the traits laid by Tueni and freeze them into this ubiquitous image. One's imagination could slip into a ludicrous thought, that if the Imam ever returns, he would reappear in the same great image we were left with since his disappearance. A mystic white halo surrounds the large turbaned head; hair 'negligently' falls over the Imam's forehead; his face, gently lit with slightly pink-coloured cheeks, denotes softness; his head is bowed with a sideways gaze, partly conveying a humble, non-confrontational gesture and partly suggesting the Imam 'soaring above' the viewer and worldly things. A delicate 'benevolent smile' is mixed with a slight frown of a pensive mind; 'enigmatic' coloured eyes, discreet yet visible beneath the partially closed lids, resonate with the divine turquoise-blue background that in turn helps in bringing forth a 'calm' but nonetheless captivating aura to the portrait.

The calligraphic logo at the bottom right of the poster stands for the word Amal, contained within a circular form, in three symbolic colours: red for blood and sacrifice, green for Islam and white for martyrdom. The red and green are seen again next to black, the colour for the perpetual mourning of the quintessential Shi'ite martyr Imam Hussein (see chapter 4), in the diagonal bands at the top-left corner of the poster. The politico-religious heritage of Shi'ism, invested with themes of oppression, struggle and martyrdom, was not absent from Mussa al-Sadr's discourse; these culturally engrained themes played a significant role in the leader's rhetoric of mobilization among the Shia community.[23] The founder of the Movement of the Disinherited also formed Amal ('Hope'), an acronym for Afwaj al-Muqawama al-Lubnaniya (Lebanese Resistance Detachments), as the movement's military arm. It was a resistance force which, in Mussa al-Sadr's words, 'responded to the call of the wounded homeland . . . in days when Israeli assaults on southern Lebanon reached their peak while authorities were not performing their duty in defending the homeland and the citizens'.[24] In the absence of the Imam and in the heat of armed conflict in Lebanon, the military wing Amal presided over the movement and did not restrict itself to Israeli resistance.

As with Jumblatt and Gemayel, the disappearance of Mussa al-Sadr led to an abundant display of his portrait-image in posters, not only in exaltation of the 'absent' leader but also in an attempt to ensure continuity of the movement under his 'spiritual' guidance and sustain the emotional bond with the admirers and partisans. In one poster, his portrait is not the main subject but the turbaned Imam mystically floats in its upper part, acquiescently watching over and 'blessing' the events that unfold beneath: his successor's leadership, his people's struggle and victory, the blessed wounded, noble martyrs and proud combatants (fig. 3.22). As previously seen in the father-and-son Jumblatt poster, here Mussa al-Sadr gives credibility to his Amal successor from 1980, Nabih Berri. 'Holder of trust from the bearer of trust' states the text on a poster where both leaders appear together in a photograph (fig. 2.20).

It has been debated whether the Imam was as influential on the Shi'ite community before his disappearance as he was after it. A large constituency of the Shia were in the seventies inclined to leftist ideologies and formed the base of Communist parties. What we can be sure of is that his figure/image surely grew in popularity and became an undisputed subject of veneration after his disappearance, more so as the eighties witnessed a rise of sectarian consciousness within Lebanese politics in general, the effect of the Iranian Revolution on the Shi'ite community in particular and the predominance of a Shi'ite religio-political discourse sustained by Hizbullah. The party featured the icon of Lebanon's Shi'ite leadership in its early formation and mobilizing efforts in an attempt to reach an audience already operating inside the Shi'ite politico-religious discourse and familiar with its signs. Many of the adherents of Hizbullah and a number of its founding members were in fact previously partisans of Amal. In some of the early Hizbullah posters, Mussa al-Sadr was represented as the Lebanese complement of Khomeini, as the 'natural' link between the Iranian model of a Shi'ite mobilization and the Lebanese one; 'Al-Sayyed Mussa al-Sadr was like a son to me,' a quote from Khomeini, features on one poster with portraits of both leaders (fig. 2.22). Here Khomeini is referring to Mussa al-Sadr's Iranian descent.

In a televised interview with Ibrahim Amin el-Sayed, a member of Hizbullah's political bureau, he is asked why Hizbullah in Lebanon has adopted political slogans by Khomeini regarding Israel and the West. He responds that these were not alien to the Lebanese condition; al-Sadr in fact used similar slogans before the Iranian Revolution.[25] One such slogan, 'Israel is an absolute evil,' has been repeatedly used by

Hizbullah in public speeches as well as posters (fig. 2.21). Because Hizbullah emerged following the 1982 Israeli invasion of Lebanon and actively resisted that occupation, in its call for collective participation it made use of reclaiming the discourse of the highly esteemed Shi'ite leader, condemning Israel and asserting the necessity of armed resistance against that enemy. The poster addressed above featuring Khomeini and al-Sadr's portraits (fig. 2.22) also illustrates a battlefield where a mujahid holds a red flag with a Koranic inscription. The image is anchored by the text at the bottom of the poster quoting Mussa al-Sadr: 'We have to form a culture of war and employ all resources in our battle with Israel',[26] a statement engrained in Hizbullah's discourse up until recent days.

يَـومَ الأرْض ٣٠ آذار ـ مارس

.D/ Unified Information / Damascus Office

منظمة التحرير الفلسطينية ـ الاعلام الموحد ـ مكتب دمشق

1.1 *Land Day, 30 March*
PLO, 1980
Abd-el-Rahman Mouzayen, 71 × 52 cm

Clockwise from top right:

1.3 *The gateway to the south will not be closed*
Committee for solidarity with Saida, 1985
Omran Kaysi, 48 × 35 cm

1.4 *Saida above the arrows of treason*
1985
Omran Kaysi, 48 × 35 cm

1.5 *The assault on Saida is an assault on
the national resistance*
1985
Omran Kaysi, 48 × 35 cm

Top left:

1.2 *The mountain's victory*
Progressive Socialist Party, 1984
Omran Kaysi, 60 × 44 cm

1.6 *Be prepared for them with all your force*
[Koranic verse]
Amal movement, mid-1980s
Rafic Charaf, 85 × 70 cm

1.7 *Immortal in the consciousness of people
and the nation*
Lebanese National Movement, 1978
Jamil Molaeb, 70 × 47 cm

لتتوحَّدالجهودمن أجل انتزاع الاستقلال وتجديده

٢٢ تشـــريـــن الثـــانـــي ١٩٨٢   الحـــزب الشـــيوعـــي اللبــنانـــي

1.8 *Let us unite our efforts in the liberation struggle,*
22 November 1982 [In commemoration of
Lebanon's Independence Day]
Lebanese Communist Party, 1982
Paul Guiragossian, 70 × 50 cm

عَامان مِن المُقاومة الوطنية اللبنَانية

المجلس الثقافي للبنان الجنوبي   ١٩٨٤/٩/٢٠

دعمًا لتحـــريـر الجنوب

تجمع الهيئات الثقافية والاعلامية لدعم تحرير الجنوب

1.9 *Two years of the Lebanese National Resistance*
Cultural Council for South Lebanon, 1984
Paul Guiragossian, 59 × 44 cm

1.10 *In support of liberating the south*
Assembly of cultural and media committees
in support of liberating the south, c.1984
Paul Guiragossian, 59 × 44 cm

1.11 *Jerusalem is ours and victory is ours*
Dar al-Fata al-Arabi, 1975
Burhan Karkutli, 91 × 66 cm

1.12 Dar al-Fata al-Arabi, 1977
Helmi el-Touni, 47 × 32 cm

1.13 *60th anniversary 1924–1984*
Lebanese Communist Party, 1984
Youssef Abdelkeh, 70 × 49 cm

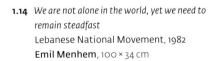

1.14 *We are not alone in the world, yet we need to remain steadfast*
Lebanese National Movement, 1982
Emil Menhem, 100 × 34 cm

1.15 *With the help of the Arab people of Libya the tobacco season was saved . . .*
Socialist Arab Union, 1980
Kameel Hawa, 72 × 50 cm

1.16 *When the Arab revolution resumes its march, Abd-el-Nasser's banners will take the lead. In commemoration of 23 July*
Socialist Arab Union, 1979
Kameel Hawa, 60 × 43 cm

ايها المقـاتـلون :
مزيداً من القبضة الفولاذية
على هذه البنادق صانعة الانتصار
القرار هو قراركم والمستقبل
والنصر لكم

1.17 *Revolution until victory. 16th anniversary of the resistance*
PLO, 1980
Ismail Shammout, 69 × 48 cm

1.18 Quote from Yasser Arafat
PLO, 1978
Seta Manoukian and Walid Safi, 180 × 60 cm

Left:
1.20 *United we shall win!*
OSPAAAL, Cuba, 1970s–80s
Anonymous, 75 × 43 cm

1.19 *Palestine*
OSPAAAL, Cuba, 1983
Rafael Enriquez, 75 × 48 cm

1.21 *Against imperialism and Zionism*
Lebanese Communist Party, 1977
Anonymous, 80 × 46 cm

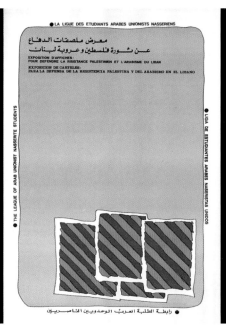

1.23 *Exhibition of posters in support of the Palestinian revolution and the Arab identity of Lebanon*
Socialist Arab Union, 1981
Kameel Hawa, 70 × 50 cm

1.22 *When we were in Sierra Maestra we got inspired by the resistance and great victory of Suez – Castro*
Socialist Arab Union, 1981
Kameel Hawa, 60 × 44 cm

1.24–1.25 Painted portraits of political leaders
mid-1980s
Muhammad Moussalli

1.26 *Following his path, our emblems will remain vigorous*
Progressive Socialist Party, *c.*1984
Mahmoud Zeineddine, 60 × 45 cm

1.27 *Jerusalem . . . here we come*
Hizbullah, *c*.1984–5
Anonymous, 70 × 50 cm

1.28 Dar al-Fata al-Arabi, *c.*1977
Helmi el-Touni, 47 × 32 cm

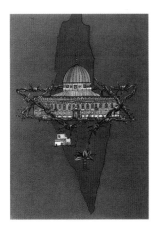

1.29 Islamic Republic of Iran,
early 1980s
Hussein Khosrojerdi

1.30 Islamic Republic of Iran,
early 1980s
Abdulfazl A'li

1.31 *A constellation/squadron of martyrs of the*
Islamic Resistance, in the western Bekaa
Islamic Resistance / Hizbullah, *c.*1985
Anonymous, 70 × 50 cm

1.32 *The martyr Ahmad Kassir. The pioneer of martyrdom
and heroism in Karbala Jabal 'Amel*
Islamic Resistance / Hizbullah, 1984
Anonymous, 70 × 50 cm

وهـل مـن شـيء
اشـرف مـن العـبور
فـوق جسرالمـوت
الى الحـيـاة
التـي تهـدف
الى إحياء الآخـرين
وإلى محض قضيتهـم
قـوة الانتصـار مع
الـزمن وإلى ترسيخ
مثال الصمود والتضحية
في نفوس المناضلين؟
كمال جنبلاط

2.1 *Is there anything more noble than crossing over the bridge of death into the life that revives others and genuinely supports their cause and that strengthens the model of resistance and sacrifice in the souls of activists? – Kamal Jumblatt*
Lebanese National Movement, 1978
Anonymous, 60 × 44 cm

JUMBLAT'S INTERNATIONAL DAY
JOURNÉE INTERNATIONALE DE JOUMBLAT

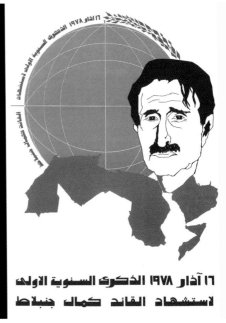

١٦ آذار ١٩٧٨ الذكرى السنوية الاولى
لاستشهاد القائد كمال جنبلاط

2.2 *1 May, Jumblatt's international day*
Lebanese National Movement, 1977
Oussama, 69 × 50 cm

2.3 *16 March 1978, the first annual commemoration of the martyr leader Kamal Jumblatt*
Lebanese National Movement, 1978
Anonymous, 70 × 50 cm

إن تزكية الدماء
أعطت مفهوماً جديداً لمعركة التحرر
كمال جنبلاط

معاً حتى النصر

2.5 *Together until victory*
Lebanese National Movement, 1978
Aref el-Rayess, 71 × 50 cm

2.4 *Offering life gave a new understanding to the*
liberation struggle – Kamal Jumblatt
Lebanese National Movement, 1979
Hassib al-Jassem, 61 × 44 cm

2.8 *Jumblatt did not die, you who call for*
submissive solutions
Lebanese National Movement, 1977
Anonymous, 50 × 70 cm

2.9 *Just like Abd-el-Nasser, Jumblatt will remain*
the symbol of an Arab revolution
Lebanese National Movement, 1977
Anonymous, 50 × 70 cm

2.6 *16 March*
Progressive Socialist Party, *c.*1985
Ghazi Saab, 70 × 50 cm

الذكرى العاشرة لاستشهاد كمال جنبلاط ١٩١٧ـ١٩٧٧

2.7 *The 10th commemoration of the martyrdom of*
Kamal Jumblatt, 1917–1977
Progressive Socialist Party, 1987
Imad Abou Ajram, 61 × 43 cm

2.10 *Jumblatt gave his life for the Palestinian cause*
and a united Arab destiny
Lebanese National Movement, 1978
Anonymous, 50 × 70 cm

2.11 *The Lebanon of Kamal Jumblatt is a fortress*
of Arab steadfastness
Lebanese National Movement, 1978
Anonymous, 50 × 70 cm

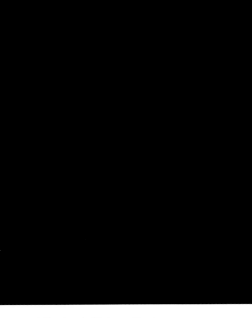

2.12 *16 March 1985. Pledge and loyalty*
Progressive Socialist Party, 1985
Mahmoud Zeineddine, 60 × 47 cm

2.13 *A pledge is a pledge*
Progressive Socialist Party,
1981
Nabil Kdouh, 65 × 50 cm

2.14 *Over time our weapons are the guarantee*
Progressive Socialist Party, 1984
Anonymous

القوات اللبنانية

لبنانا بحاجة اليك
أنت

2.15 *Our Lebanon needs you, YOU*
Lebanese Forces, *c.*1983
Pierre Sadek, 66 × 48 cm

2.16 Portrait of Bashir Gemayel when elected president
Lebanese Kataeb, 1982
Varoujan, 95 × 64 cm

2.17 *23 August*
Lebanese Forces, 1983
Pierre Sadek, 66 × 44 cm

2.18 *14 September*
Lebanese Forces, 1983
Raidy, 66 × 47 cm

2.19 Portrait of Mussa al-Sadr
Amal movement, 1978
Anonymous, 69 × 49 cm

حامل الأمانة من صاحب الأمانة

2.20 *Holder of trust from the bearer of trust*
Amal movement, c.1980
Anonymous, 42 × 60 cm

إسرائيل شرّ مطلق

2.21 *Israel is an absolute evil*
Hizbullah, 1985
Muhammad Ismail
60 × 22 cm

2.22 *Al-Sayyed Mussa al-Sadr was like a son to me – Khomeini.*
We have to form a culture of war and employ all resources
in our battle with Israel – Mussa al-Sadr
Hizbullah, c.1985
Anonymous, 64 × 42 cm

3.1 53 years for the renaissance and unity of society
and for liberating the nation from Zionist and
foreign occupation
Syrian Social Nationalist Party, 1985
Roger Sawaya, 68 × 31 cm

3.2 Israel wants our land without people. Protection
of land. Protection of existence and destiny
Syrian Social Nationalist Party, 1977
Diab, 70 × 50 cm

3.3 1 March. The birth of national consciousness
and the will for victory
Syrian Social Nationalist Party, 1970s
Anonymous, 58 × 42 cm

3.4 *44 years in the service of Lebanon*
Lebanese Kataeb, 1980
Pierre Sadek, 66 × 47 cm

الكتائب اللبنانية

3.5 *44 years in the service of Lebanon*
Lebanese Kataeb, 1980
Wajih Nahle, 68 × 50 cm

3.6 *60th anniversary. The sun rises from the south*
Lebanese Communist Party, 1984
Anonymous, 68 × 48 cm

3.7 *60th anniversary*
Lebanese Communist Party, 1984
Anonymous, 68 × 48 cm

أوّلُ آذار
مَولِدُ المُقَاوَمَةِ القَومِيَّةِ الوَاعِيَة
في أمَّةٍ ظنَّها أعداؤها مُنقرِضَة

الذكرى الواحدة والثمانين لميلاد سعاده مؤسس الحزب السوري القومي الاجتماعي

3.8 *1 March. The birth of the national resistance in a nation*
thought to be extinct by its enemies. The 81st anniversary
of Saadeh's birthday, the founder of the SSNP
Syrian Social Nationalist Party, 1977
Tammouz Knayzeh and Camil Baraka, 66 × 46 cm

Opposite page:

3.10 *Commemoration of Gamal Abd-el-Nasser's*
birthday. A green memory in days of drought
Socialist Arab Union, 1979
Helmi el-Touni, 61 × 45 cm

3.9 *8 July, commemoration of Saadeh's martyrdom.*
I die yet my party remains
Syrian Social Nationalist Party, 1980s
Roger Sawaya, 63 × 30 cm

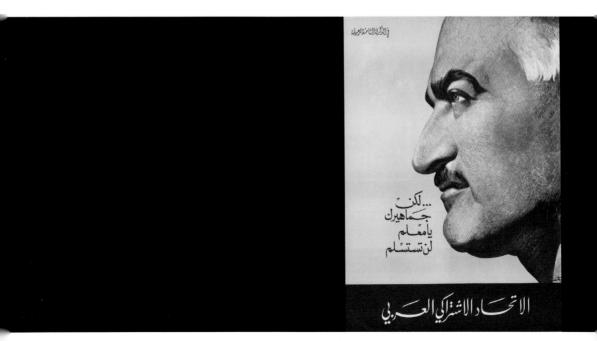

3.11 *. . . But your followers will not surrender. The 8th commemoration of Gamal Abd-el-Nasser's passing* Socialist Arab Union, 1978
Anonymous, 69 × 49 cm

3.12 *13 April, the dawn of freedom*
Lebanese Forces, *c.*1983
Raidy, 48 × 23 cm

3.13 *13 April*
Lebanese Forces, *c.*1983
Anonymous, 44 × 29 cm

3.14 *. . . Continuing the procession*
Lebanese Forces, 1983
Pierre Sadek, 70 × 50 cm

3.15 *This is what the Zionists have done in Deir Yassin in 1948 . . . and this is what the Kataeb gangs have done in Ain el-Rummaneh in 1975*
Arab Liberation Front, *c.*1975–6
Anonymous, 48 × 69 cm

3.16 *On the 9th commemoration of one of their most atrocious massacres; we salute you who executed the people's judgment over the butcher. 13 April 1984*
Friends of Habib Shartuni, 1984
Anonymous, 47 × 32 cm

3.17 13 June. They sought for it to be our grave . . .
it was instead our dawn
Marada, 1979
Anonymous, 40 × 30 cm

3.18 Tal el-Za'tar, the cradle of heroism and martyrdom
PLO, 1976
Anonymous, 70 × 50 cm

3.19 The Maslakh has fallen yet the will to resist did
not and will not fall. 2nd commemoration
Socialist Arab Union, 1978
Anonymous, 70 × 50 cm

3.20 *2nd commemoration of the Sabra and Shatila massacre*
Palestinian National Alliance, 1984
Ihsan Farhat, 70 × 50 cm

3.21 *Zahleh. 2 April 1983*
Lebanese Forces, 1983
Pierre Sadek, 66 × 45 cm

3.22 *Lift hegemony and block Zionism, 6 February*
Amal movement, 1984
Nabil Kdouh, 70 × 50 cm

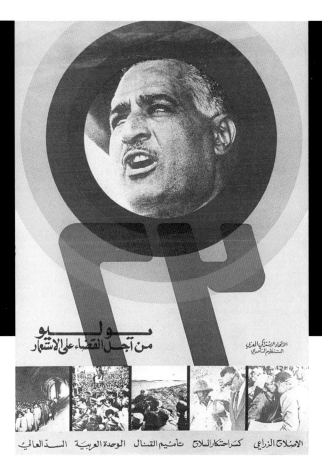

3.23 *23 July. For the abolition of colonialism*
Socialist Arab Union, 1977
Anonymous, 79 × 55 cm

3.24 *7 April. One Arab nation with an eternal message*
Organization of the Arab Socialist Baath
Party in Lebanon, 1987
Anonymous, 60 × 46 cm

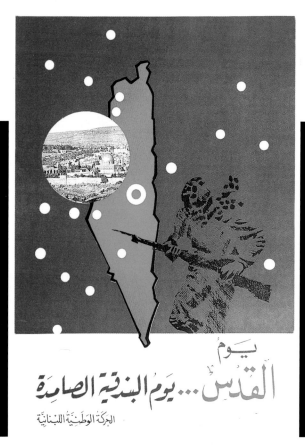

3.25 *Jerusalem Day . . . the day of the steadfast rifle*
Lebanese National Movement, 1978
Anonymous, 60 × 40 cm

3.26 *We have one policy for peace: that the enemies
of this nation give it back its due rights. 15 May,
commemoration of the division of Palestine and
the establishment of the Israeli state*
Syrian Social Nationalist Party, c.1977
Tammouz Knayzeh and Camil Baraka,
50 × 34 cm

3.27 *Muslim Woman's Day*
Hizbullah / Islamic Women
Committee, 1984
Anonymous

3.28 *Jerusalem . . . here we come. Every Muslim has to*
prepare himself to confront Israel . . . and Jerusalem
will ultimately return to Muslims – Khomeini
Hizbullah, *c.*1984
Anonymous, 74 × 51 cm

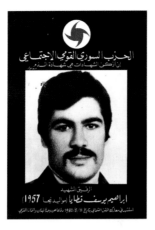

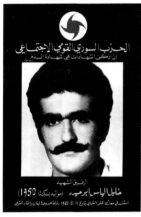

4.1–4.4 Syrian Social Nationalist Party, 1980
Anonymous, 56 × 40 cm

4.5–4.6 Socialist Arab Union, 1981
Anonymous, 58 × 46 cm

4.7–4.8 Lebanese National Resistance Front /
Organization of the Arab Socialist
Baath Party in Lebanon, 1985
Anonymous, 45 × 30 cm

4.9 Lebanese Communist
Party, 1989
Anonymous, 50 × 23 cm

شهيد جبهة المقاومة الوطنية اللبنانية
الرفيق جمال ساطي
بطل عملية تفجير مقر الحاكم العسكري الإسرائيلي في حاصبيا

«لا يهمني متى وكيف سأموت، بل كل ما يهمني هو أن
تبقى الثورة متقدة في كل أنحاء الأرض في إبتسام العالم بكل
نقط فوق أجساد الفقراء»

استشهد في عملية بطولية في ١٩٨٥/٨/٦ ضد قوات الاحتلال الإسرائيلي وعملائه

شهيدة جبهة المقاومة الوطنية اللبنانية
البطلة وفاء نور الدين

«لا طريق الا طريق المقاومة الوطنية»
ـ من وصية الشهيدة البطلة وفاء نور الدين ـ

استشهدت في عملية بطولية في ٨٥/٥/٩ ضد قوات الاحتلال الإسرائيلي وعملائه

شهيدة جبهة المقاومة الوطنية اللبنانية
لؤلؤة البقاع لولا الياس عبود

«جبهة المقاومة الوطنية هي الطريق الوحيد
للتحرير والتوحيد والتغيير الديمقراطي»
ـ من طلب انتساب الشهيدة لولا الياس عبود الى الجبهة ـ

استشهدت في عملية بطولية في ٨٥/٤/٢١ ضد قوات الاحتلال الإسرائيلي وعملائه

4.10–4.12 Lebanese National Resistance Front /
Lebanese Communist Party, 1985
Anonymous, 57 × 27 cm, 68 × 28 cm

4.15–4.17
Hizbullah, 1986
Anonymous, 54 × 38 cm

4.13–4.14
National Liberal Party, c.1976
Anonymous

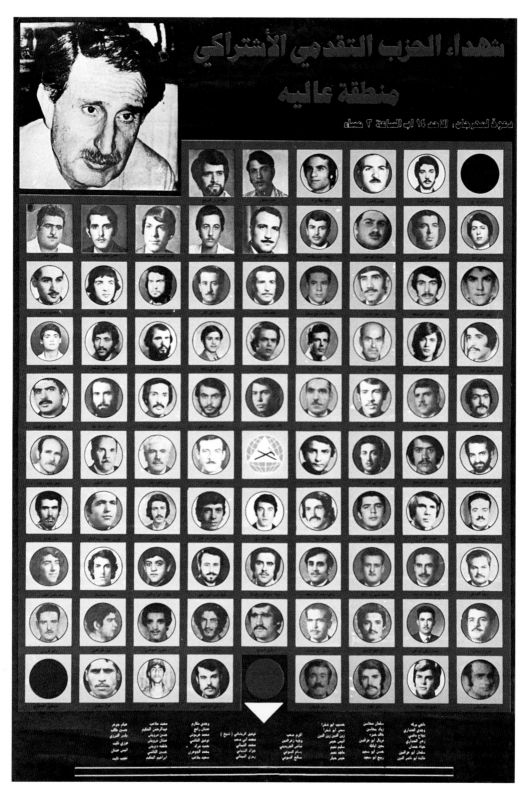

4.18 *The martyrs of the PSP, Aley*
Progressive Socialist Party, c.1983
Anonymous, 82 × 56 cm

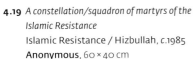

4.19 *A constellation/squadron of martyrs of the*
Islamic Resistance
Islamic Resistance / Hizbullah, *c.*1985
Anonymous, 60 × 40 cm

4.20 *From the Mina [northern port city in Tripoli] to*
the nation, 1924–1986
Lebanese Communist Party, 1986
Anonymous, 62 × 45 cm

4.21 *16 December 1986 – 54 years of building and*
struggle. The heroic martyrs who fell in the battle
of national pride in the northern Matn
Syrian Social Nationalist Party, 1986
Roger Sawaya, 70 × 48 cm

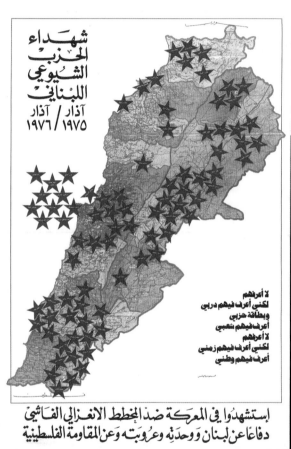

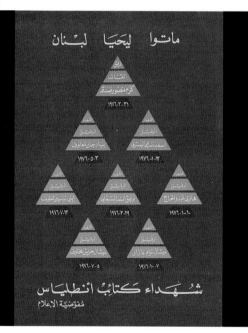

4.22 *Martyrs of the Lebanese Communist Party, March 1975–March 1976; martyrs in the battle against the fascist isolationist plan in defence of Lebanon, its unity, Arab identity and in defence of the Palestinian resistance*
Lebanese Communist Party, 1976
Anonymous, 96 × 66 cm

4.23 *They died for Lebanon to live. The martyrs of the Kataeb in Antelias*
Lebanese Kataeb, 1976
Anonymous, 70 × 48 cm

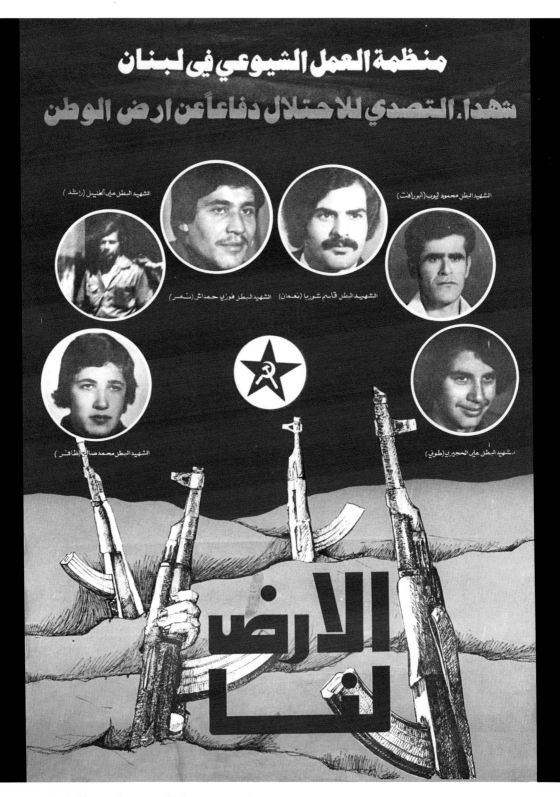

4.24 *The land is ours. The martyrs of defiance to occupation in defence of the nation's land*
Organization of Communist Action in Lebanon, c.1980–1
Anonymous, 81 × 55 cm

4.25 *Toumat Niha's high-quality operation*
Islamic Resistance / Hizbullah, 1987
Muhammad Ismail, 70 × 50 cm

4.26 *The martyred leader Ahmad al-Meer al-Ayoubi (Abu Hassan), member of the political bureau of the Lebanese Communist Party*
Lebanese Communist Party, 1979
Anonymous, 71 × 49 cm

4.27 *The 2nd commemoration of the first martyrdom operation in Jabal 'Amel. The first in the reign of heroism, the pioneer of martyrdom operations; the happy martyr Ahmad Kassir 'Haydar'; the destroyer of the headquarters of the Israeli military governor in Sour*
Islamic Resistance / Hizbullah, 1984
Anonymous, 70 × 50 cm

4.28 *The groom of the south. The martyr Bilal Fahs*
Amal movement, 1984
Nabil Kdouh, 60 × 42 cm

4.29 *The hero of the Wimpy operation, the martyr comrade Khaled Alwan*
Lebanese National Resistance Front / Syrian Social Nationalist Party, 1982
Anonymous, 70 × 45 cm

4.30 *In the first annual commemoration of Sana' Mehaidli. 9 May 1986. The week of the resistant woman*
Lebanese National Resistance Front / Syrian Social Nationalist Party, 1986
M. Haydar, 70 × 50 cm

العَدَوّ الإسْرائيلي هوعَدَوّ أمّتي وَلن نَدَعُه يَرتَاح
وجدي

أنا الآنَ مَزروعَةٌ في ترابِ الجنوبِ أسقيهِ مِن دَمي
سناء

بِسِلاَح الإرادة والتَصميم والمقاومة سَنَنتَصِر
مريم

إن طريقَ تحريرِ فلسطينَ ليسَت منحرفة وليسَت ملتوية، ولا يَمرُّ عبرَ
عواصمِ كامبْ ديفيد، بَل إنها تمرُّ أولاً وأخيراً مِن فوهَة البندقيّة المقاتلة
قائدة عملية نهاريا الشهيد محمّد محمود

4.31 *The Israeli enemy is the enemy of my nation and we will not let it rest – Wajdi*
Lebanese National Resistance Front / Syrian Social Nationalist Party, 1985
Anonymous, 61 × 45 cm

4.32 *I am now planted in the south, I soak its earth with my blood – Sana'*
Lebanese National Resistance Front / Syrian Social Nationalist Party, 1985
Anonymous, 60 × 45 cm

4.33 *With the arms of will, determination and resistance we shall be victorious – Maryam*
Lebanese National Resistance Front / Syrian Social Nationalist Party, 1985
Anonymous, 60 × 45 cm

4.34 *The road to the liberation of Palestine is not bent, and does not pass through Camp David; it passes first and foremost through armed struggle – the leader of the Naharaya operation, the martyr Muhammad Mahmoud*
Lebanese National Resistance Front / Syrian Social Nationalist Party, 1986
Anonymous, 60 × 45 cm

سنعبر وسط بحر من الدماء لنصل إلى نصر الله المؤزّر

المقاومة الاسلامية   الذكرى السنوية الاولى لاستشهاد الشيخ المجاهد راغب حرب

4.35 *We will cross a sea of blood to reach God's blessed victory*
Islamic Resistance / Hizbullah, 1985
Anonymous, 70 × 50 cm

يا راغب أبا الحرب، عهداً لدمك الحسيني الرافض أن نبقى راغبين
بقتال الصهاينه حتى القضاء على إسرائيل

4.36 2nd commemoration
of the assassination of
Sheikh Ragheb Harb
Hizbullah, 1986
Merhi Merhi, 40 × 60 cm

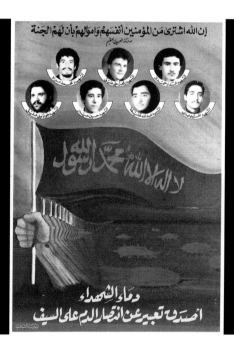

إن الله اشترى من المؤمنين أنفسهم وأموالهم بأن لهم الجنة

لا اله الا الله محمد رسول الله

ودماء الشهداء
أصدق تعبير عن انتصار الدم على السيف

4.37 The blood of martyrs is the most honest
expression of blood vanquishing the sword
Islamic Resistance / Hizbullah, mid-1980s
Anonymous, 70 × 50 cm

المقاومة الاسلامية
عزنا... وفخرنا وسيد الشهداء... منارة دربنا

4.38 The Islamic Resistance. Our glory . . . our pride and
the Prince of Martyrs . . . the guide to our path
Islamic Resistance / Hizbullah, c.1986
Merhi Merhi, 70 × 50 cm

4.39 *The martyr of Islam Taysir Kdouh*
Islamic Resistance / Hizbullah, 1985
Anonymous, 64 × 43 cm

4.40 *God's victorious Lion. The martyr*
Hajj Nassar Nassar
Islamic Resistance / Hizbullah, 1980s
Adel Selman, 69 × 48 cm

4.41 *A resistant leader . . . His jihad is your pride and*
his blood is your freedom
Islamic Resistance / Hizbullah, 1988
Muhammad Ismail, 60 × 43 cm

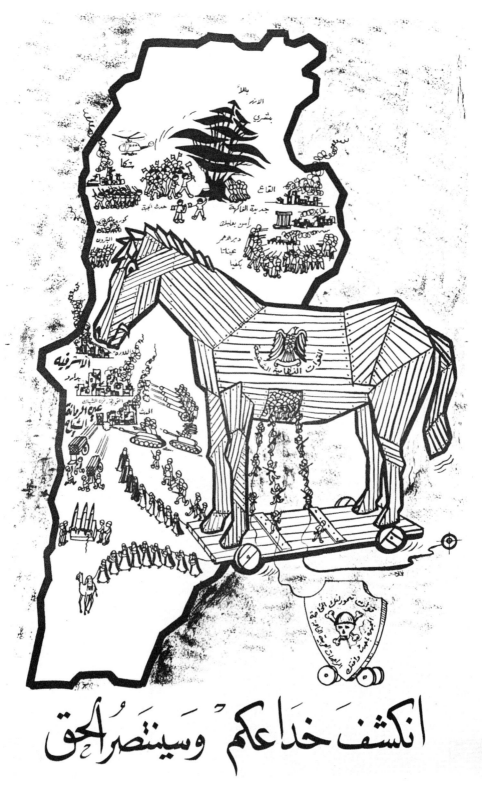

5.1 *Your tricks are uncovered and justice will prevail*
c.1978–9
Anonymous, 70 × 50 cm

5.2 *The murderer . . . the combatant*
Lebanese Kataeb, 1983
Anonymous, 50 × 70 cm

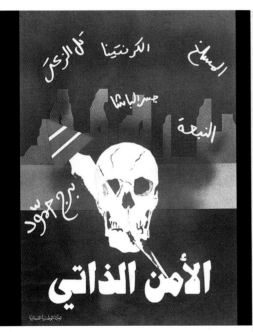

5.3 *Self-security*
Lebanese National Movement, 1979
Anonymous, 64 × 47 cm

5.4 *On 21 March 1976, the Murabitun destroyed the symbol of fascist treason and took an oath of continuing the journey at whatever cost –*
Ibrahim Koleilat
Independent Nasserist Movement – Murabitun, 1977
Anonymous, 70 × 50 cm

5.5 *The Kataeb rule: Preacher of destruction, guardian of the dollar*
Union of Muslim 'Ulama, 1985
Anonymous

5.6 *1st annual commemoration of Houmin massacre*
Islamic Resistance / Hizbullah, 1986
Muhammad Ismail, 60 × 40 cm

5.7 *The new Nazism passed through South Lebanon*
Ministry of the South, *c.*1983–5
Ibn al-Junoub, 70 × 50 cm

5.8 *We will resist*
Lebanese National Resistance Front /
Ministry of the South, 1983
Nazem Irani, 64 × 48 cm

5.9 Lebanese National Movement, *c.*1981
Anonymous, 64 × 48 cm

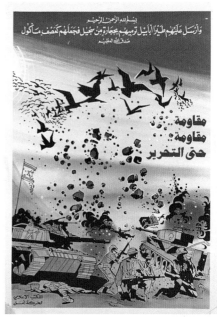

5.10 *Martyrdom is a pledge and commitment for victory and liberation*
Amal movement, mid-1980s
Nabil Kdouh, 60 × 40 cm

5.11 *Resistance . . . resistance . . . until liberation*
Amal movement, mid-1980s
Nabil Kdouh, 69 × 50 cm

5.12 *The American–Israeli 'peace' in Lebanon*
Organization of Communist Action in Lebanon, c.1978–9
Helmi el-Touni, 62 × 42 cm

5.14 *If you love it, work for it*
Tanzim, 1977
Anonymous, 59 × 44 cm

5.13 *The world is asleep while Ain el-Rummaneh stays awake*
c.1978–9
Anonymous, 69 × 50 cm

5.15 *We will build with those who stay*
c.1978–9
Anonymous, 50 × 36 cm

5.16 *Towards independence*
Lebanese Forces, 1980
Anonymous, 49 × 35 cm

5.17 *The Arab sun rises from the south*
Lebanese National Movement, c.1980
Anonymous, 64 × 49 cm

5.18 *Steadfast in the south*
Independent Nasserist Movement – Murabitun, 1980
Anonymous, 69 × 48 cm

5.19 *The south*
Lebanese National Movement, *c.*1978–9
Anonymous, 82 × 55 cm

رفيقي المقاوم ؛

① امام طلتك ، تنحني الشمس ؛ وعند وقع أقدام بطولاتك ، يسجد التاريخ .

② دماء رفاقك الشهداء ، ستحفر بأحرف من نور في كل قلب وعلى كل جبين .

③ فمن يموت في سبيل حرية الانسان ، خير ممن يبقى حيا بانتظار الموت .

④ رفيقي ، أنت في الجبل صنعت المجد ، والتاريخ سجل .

⑤ بإيمانك ، حاربت من أجل قضية أثمن وأقدس وأعمق حتى من البقاء .

⑥ بصمودك ، حافظت على وجودنا المسيحي الحر الكريم في هذا المحيط .

⑦ بمقاومتك ، يتحدى ويصمد النوع في وجه الكثرة .

⑧ أنت المقاوم العنيد ؛ من بلا الى الاشرفية ، من قنات الى زحلة . من المطلة الى بجدون فدير القمر ... تبقى رمزا للعيش الحر .

⑨ أنت درع شعبنا المسيحي ، وسور حزيته ، وضمان ديمومته ، بسقوطك ، يسقط .

⑩ ان بقاءنا اذا ، رهـن بإيمانك وصمودك .

رفيقي المقاوم ؛

⑪ أنت الشهادة للحق الذي هو لبنان ، والدم التوقيع .

بشير حي فينا
ليبقى لبنانا

5.21 *My resisting comrade [. . .] Bashir lives in us so that our Lebanon remains*
Lebanese Forces, 1983
Anonymous, 70 × 50 cm

5.20 *Comrade . . . you are heroism, you are faith, with you Lebanon remains. Bashir lives in us*
Lebanese Forces, 1983
Kasparian, 70 × 50 cm

5.23 Logo: *Our mountain: man, land and heritage*
Lebanese Forces, 1984
Anonymous

5.24 *The Christmas of 'our mountain' children, 23 December 1984*
Lebanese Forces, 1984
Anonymous

5.22 *April 13 1984 . . . Here we remain*
Lebanese Forces, 1984
Anonymous, 44 × 35 cm

5.25 *The mountain's upbringing*
Progressive Socialist Party, 1984
Anonymous, 64 × 42 cm

3

Commemoration

Commemoration is a common worldwide practice, normalized into our everyday life through national holidays, memorial ceremonies and the like. These official dates call for collective celebrations or grieving in memory of selected moments marked in history and legitimized by religious and secular state institutions. These moments are lived annually, intensified by the collective performance of symbolically loaded rituals with narratives that rouse our emotions of collectivity. 'We' are yearly comforted that 'we' are not left alone with 'our' memories; 'we' shall sing together, march together, pray together, hold candles together, hold a moment of silence, love, hate and cry together . . . These emotional acts of collective remembrance conceal the various kinds of power that underlie the way narratives of a particular past are inscribed into 'our' collective memory. 'Collective memory is not an inert and passive thing,' Edward Said notes, 'but a field of activity in which past events are selected, reconstructed, maintained, modified, and endowed with political meaning.'[1]

In the context of Lebanon's civil war, nationalism was a contested terrain, subject to hegemonic struggle by the various political communities under formation and transformation during wartime. A consensual national identity was challenged by the constructions of multiple and antagonistic political identities, each constituting its own collective memory, in which constructions of national history as well as narratives of the war events are written into a community's political discourse. Many posters have been made to commemorate events that are significant to a given political community and published by its party or movement. Marked annually, these dates got institutionalized and their narratives eventually materialize in people's imaginaries. The 15 years of war, witnessing many warring factions and antagonistic political communities, left us with a plethora of commemorative posters, a great number of dates to 'remember', far too many intertwining and conflicting narratives to fathom.

In times of political and armed conflict wherein the well-being of a collective 'we' is threatened, political events command great collective emotional legitimacy. These dates range from events that are specific to the party or political community, such as the founding date and founder's birthday, to regional events to which the community ascribes its struggle. The commemorative poster provides a moment during wartime to recall and affirm the party's continuity in struggle and its ideological position. The historical narratives represented in the poster can symbolically write and rewrite meanings that are significant to a present moment in the unfolding of the war. A number of commemorative posters also address wartime events, 'victorious battles' and 'violent massacres'. The narratives of such events were a contested terrain, subject to political struggle and symbolic appropriation by the various political communities. Conflicting constructions of wartime history were thus written into the different communities' political discourse. The politics of commemoration here joins the battle over meaning and history.

The founding of the party

Not all political parties attach the same great importance to commemorating their founding date as the Lebanese Communist Party, the Syrian Social Nationalist Party and the Lebanese Kataeb Party. These three parties are the oldest in Lebanon. They were founded (respectively in 1925, 1932 and 1936) during the creation of Greater Lebanon, under French colonial rule, as a national territory divided from Syria (declared in 1920). They share the legitimacy of a senior political establishment – the age is clearly emphasized in some of their posters, 44th, 45th, 53rd and 60th anniversaries – yet are in conflict ideologically. In the three cases, continuity in struggle, commitment and sacrifice are evident in text and image, yet the cause and narratives vary tremendously.

The ideological discord is most obvious in the posters of the SSNP and the Kataeb, with their distinct national imaginaries. In a poster commemorating its 53rd anniversary in 1985, the SSNP chose the theme of a natural landscape depicting the rising morning sun – a scenery typical to the physical geography of Lebanon, while also related to Lebanon's political geography, as the sun rises from behind the eastern mountain chain that defines the border with Syria (fig. 3.1). The SSNP logo, a white circle enclosing a red cyclone shape, *al-zawba'a*, vigorously rises from behind the eastern Lebanese mountains. Its energy, like that of the sun, radiates across the landscape. One of the key objectives of the SSNP, since its inception, is the building of Greater Syria, referred to geographically in the literature of the SSNP as the Fertile Crescent: a natural geographic environment that unites Lebanon with Syria, Jordan, Palestine, the northern parts of Iraq and Cyprus (see map of Greater Syria in fig. 3.3). Antun Saadeh, founder of the SSNP, dismissed Lebanese nationalism and argued that it had no historical or sociological foundation. The Lebanese people, he claimed, could not be separated from Syria, for they had always been a part of its history and community.[2] The poster image reinstates the party's ideology as the dawn of a movement towards the accomplishment of the Syrian nation; a future state based, in Saadeh's words, on four pillars: freedom, duty, order and force, which are symbolized by the four sides of the SSNP emblem.[3] The image is anchored by the title '53 years for the renaissance and unity of society and for liberating the nation from Zionist and foreign occupation'. 'Nation' here means the greater Syrian nation; the title recalls the SSNP's struggle against colonial occupation and the subsequent division of Syria into separate states, among them the establishment of the Israeli state. With this poster title, the SSNP gives historical legitimacy to its resistance in 1985 to Israeli occupation of Lebanon, by tying it to a seemingly consistent narrative of national liberation struggle since its own inception in 1932.

Lebanese nationalism antagonizes pan-Syrianism in the Kataeb posters that commemorate '44 years in the service of Lebanon'. On one of the 44th-anniversary posters a calligraphic rendering of this title takes the form of the party's logo: a graphic abstraction of the cedar tree, the central symbol on the Lebanese flag (fig. 3.5). The commitment to Lebanon as a nation is further exemplified in a second poster where the flag of the party and that of the Lebanese state are interconnected and form one unified whole; the Kataeb side of the flag sheds blood 'in the service of Lebanon' (fig. 3.4). The image clearly affirms the Kataeb's Lebanese nationalist position and its proclaimed role as 'surrogate and defender' of the Lebanese state, its sovereignty, institutions and symbols.[4] Among the different communities that made up the Lebanese nation, the Maronites (who comprise the overwhelming majority of the Kataeb party) were the ones to find in it a great degree of national political identification and to hold a protective attitude towards the Lebanese state. (Greater) Lebanon as a modern nation with its present boundaries was in fact conceived as an extension of the Mount Lebanon district, where a Lebanese identity was given its first legal definition in the nineteenth century.[5] That sense of identity developed mainly among the Maronites who were the overwhelming majority, and therefore governed the Mount Lebanon district and saw in it a national homeland.[6] The narrative of the poster image gets completed as we see the flags occupying the centre of a silhouetted profile of Pierre Gemayel, the founder and leader of the Kataeb party, who advocated since its inception in 1936 a Lebanese nationalist position against the adversaries of the then newly established state.

On the other hand, the Lebanese Communist Party does not proclaim any nationalist ideology in the many posters that celebrate its 60th anniversary (in 1984), yet it alludes to a national engagement as it extends its commitment to the resistance of occupation (figs 3.6–3.7). In much of Lebanon's wartime iconography, barbed wire refers to inaccessible borders and occupied territories, namely South Lebanon under Israeli occupation. The dripping blood of the Communist star, symbolic of martyrdom and sacrifice, cuts through the barbed wire in one of the LCP posters to lyrically reaffirm the Communist Party's active participation in the National Resistance Front against the Israeli occupation of Lebanon.

The birthday and death of the party founder

Themes of leadership and commemoration in Lebanon's political posters are very much interrelated. The dates of birth, death or assassination of political party founders were profusely the subject of commemoration in posters. A poster by the SSNP marks Antun Saadeh's birth on 1 March (fig. 3.8) and another mourns his 'martyrdom' on 8 July (fig. 3.9). In the aftermath of the 1948 establishment of the Israeli state and annexation of Palestine, Antun Saadeh called for armed rebellion in Lebanon. Accused of plotting against state security, Saadeh was sentenced to death by a military tribunal and executed on 8 July 1949. In addition to the date of establishment of the party, these dates are the main subjects of regular annual commemoration by the SSNP. The two above-mentioned posters are equally bold and direct in their graphic representation; the strict use of the colours red, black and white, the graphic abstraction of an eagle, and the drawn profile of Saadeh inscribed in the shape of a blood drop constitute highly symbolic imagery implying sharpness, power and sacrifice, virtues meant to be followed by 'his' party's adherents.

'1 March. The birth of the national resistance . . .' In this poster title the birth of Saadeh's natural body is united with that of the party's body politic; 'I die yet my party remains' – his body politic remains through *his* party beyond the death of his natural body, as the second poster affirms. The immortality of Saadeh's body politic, referred to in this set of posters, is tied to the phenomenon of glorification of the leader in the history of modern political propaganda; it has characterized the subject of posters for Hitler and Mussolini in Nazi and Fascist propaganda and under totalitarian leadership such as that of Stalin.[7]

Strong allegiance to personality cults is in fact a recurrent phenomenon in Lebanon. As was thoroughly addressed in chapter 2, with the rise of intercommunal conflict, several leaders emerged as the custodians of their respective political communities and their icons competed over the dominion of Lebanese public space. It is not surprising that dates specific to the party's founder are commemorated as much as, if not more than, the date of foundation of the party. In fact, among the above-mentioned examples of commemorative posters, the party's establishment has mostly been tied to the exaltation of its founder. Commemoration of leaders' personal dates, such as their birthdates, renders the personal/private date a collective political one. On many such commemorative posters the dates in graphic numbers occupy the central subject without any added information on what that date stands for. It would seem as an interpellation to an audience familiar with these dates and their symbolic political significance.

Nasserist organizations in Lebanon have produced a number of posters that celebrate the Egyptian president (1954–70) Gamal Abd-el-Nasser's birthday on 15 January and that mourn the death of the 'revolutionary Arab leader' on 28 September. A poster celebrating Abd-el-Nasser's birthday commemorates simultaneously the fifth anniversary of the Socialist Arab Union in a hopeful and gay representation of nature's fertility, while the text unexpectedly concludes 'in days of drought' (fig. 3.10). The poster commemorating his death is equally hopeful; it asserts popular continuity of Nasserism, yet again despite the 'drought', clarified here as 'surrender' (fig. 3.11). The reassuring tone in spite of dire circumstances can be better understood in the context in which these posters were done. They were published respectively in January 1979 and in September 1978, following the Camp David peace treaty between Egypt and Israel in September 1978, signed by Anwar el-Sadat (president of Egypt 1970–81) to the dismay of many Nasserists and other popular movements in the Arab world. The posters point to Sadat's submissive acts and affirm the continuity of a Nasserist popularity discontent with the peace treaty.

Violence remembered/forgotten

> All profound changes in consciousness, by their very nature, bring with them characteristic amnesias. Out of such oblivions, in specific historical circumstances, spring narratives . . . To serve the narrative purpose, these violent deaths [exemplary suicides, poignant martyrdoms, assassinations, executions, wars and holocausts] must be remembered/forgotten as 'our own'.[8]

There is no official text that consensually explains how and why the civil war in Lebanon started, yet there is a consensus on an official date, 13 April 1975, that marks the beginning of the armed conflict. The date corresponds to a violent incident that arguably ignited the civil war, in which the Lebanese Kataeb party militiamen attacked a bus carrying Palestinian passengers, killing about 33 of them, presumably in retaliation for an attempt on the life of the party leader that same day. The bus was passing across Ain el-Rummaneh, an area in the eastern Christian sector of Beirut's periphery, situated on the green line that ultimately divided the capital into two sectors.

13 April 1975 has been the main subject of commemorative posters by the Lebanese Forces (figs 3.12–3.13). The Lebanese Forces were formed in 1976 as a unified armed force of the Lebanese Front, which included the Lebanese Kataeb and other right-wing Lebanese nationalist parties. Seeing that the Lebanese Forces' emergence is contingent to the outbreak of the war, it becomes evident why they gave importance to that date unlike other political factions. On 13 April, the Lebanese Forces commemorate their formation and recall their mission, similar to how other parties celebrate their founding date.

'13 April, the dawn of freedom' titles a poster issued by the Lebanese Forces circa 1983. The image, featuring two combatants in action, completes the poster message – 'the dawn of freedom' through military activity. A radiating energy emanates from the combatants, extending beyond the edges of the poster. They are metaphorically represented as a sun that has began its natural daily course – 'the dawn' – in 1975 to accomplish freedom. 'Freedom' can be understood within the front's discourse of a sovereign Lebanon, free of 'foreign' armed forces, namely the Palestinian resistance and Syrian troops. The poster was issued in a period following the evacuation of the Palestinian Liberation Organization and the Syrian army from Beirut in September 1982. Yet just a few weeks later, Beirut was invaded by Israel. Lebanon endured in 1982 the invasion of its territories from its southern end up to its capital city. The accomplished 'freedom' that the poster suggests does not seem to be hindered by the Israeli occupation of Lebanese territories.

Aside from the many posters issued by the Lebanese Forces in commemoration of 13 April 1975, I have come across only two posters produced by other factions that address the same date and historical event. The first was issued by the Arab Liberation Front, a faction of the PLO, and links two violent events, disconnected in time and place, into one narrative (fig. 3.15). The apparent link is the civilian victims, as the photographs bluntly document. The text affirms: 'This' – the violent deaths in the photographs – 'is what the Zionists have done in Deir Yassin in 1948 . . . and this is what the Kataeb gangs have done in Ain el-Rummaneh in 1975'. The poster through a tight interplay of text and photography affirms that the victim is *still* the same: the Palestinian people. The authors of the poster claim *this is how it was in 1948* and *this is how it still is in 1975*. The hostile image of 'the Zionist enemy' shared in the collective imaginary of the displaced Palestinian population is reinstated in this poster and transposed onto the Kataeb. Deir Yassin was the beginning of the Palestinian *nakba* (tragedy); by correlation, Ain el-Rummaneh, the poster implies, might be the beginning of yet another project of annihilation of the Palestinians. By collapsing two distinct events into one continuous narrative, the poster message ideologically connects the 'aggressors', Kataeb and Zionist, as equally threatening enemies of the Palestinian people. 13 April 1975 is condemned as a violent event in the Palestinian poster; it is inscribed within the community's discourse of perpetual threats and suffering.

I return to another poster issued in 1983 by the Lebanese Forces (fig. 3.14). It builds on the 13 April date to evoke the memory of Bashir Gemayel, the founder and military leader of the Lebanese Forces. Gemayel was assassinated in September 1982, just after he was elected president of Lebanon. Around 1983, many posters were produced to mobilize the Lebanese Forces combatants, building on their memory and esteem for their lost idol (see chapter 2). '. . . Continuing the procession' is the title of the poster: the journey to be continued is illustrated by the act of passing the rifle from one fighter to the other. The soldier in the foreground with a recognizable face is Bashir Gemayel in his LF military attire, his arm muscles flexed as he passes the rifle on to a generic figure of an LF fighter. The fighter has his back turned; he receives the rifle and heads upwards, outside the frame of the poster. We imagine him running and handing it to another similar soldier, and so on, 'continuing the procession' initiated by Bashir Gemayel, until the ultimate destination is reached. In other words, continuing the course of military combat to reach 'freedom' as expressed in the previous LF poster.

The myth of national hero constructed around Bashir Gemayel by his community was not uncontested. In fact, his many Lebanese adversaries regarded him as a traitor who allied with their national enemy, Israel. His coming to presidency, in conjunction with the Israeli invasion and occupation of Lebanon, was a distressing fact to many political communities, which publicly voiced their discontent to say the least and challenged the authority of the myth around his persona. This brings me to the second poster commemorating 13 April issued by the opposing camp. The poster was published in 1984 on the occasion of the ninth commemoration of 13 April; it is signed by 'friends of Habib Shartuni' (fig. 3.16). Although it does not hold the signature of a specific party, the side that issued it is obvious. Habib Shartuni is a member of the Syrian Social Nationalist Party in Lebanon. He was behind the bomb blast that killed Bashir Gemayel in 1982 and was eventually arrested and put in prison. The poster does not deny his act, but rather honours it. Its title refers to a moral judgment laid by the people to name Bashir Gemayel as 'butcher' rather than victim. On

13 April, the poster recalls, nine years later, the Ain el-Rummaneh incident as 'one of their most atrocious massacres'. The title incriminates Bashir Gemayel as the indirect perpetrator of these crimes, thereby deserving punishment, and salutes Shartuni for having executed the people's judgment. The poster thus switches the roles between victim and criminal by subverting the legality of the official sentence on Shartuni to give instead moral legitimacy to his act.

13 April is celebrated by the Lebanese Forces as an awakening to national salvation, while the event is remembered and condemned as an act of violence by the opposing camp. The antagonism between the two sets of posters is clearly visible just by the contrast of colours – white and bright colours versus black. In each of the commemorative posters, the meanings of the historical event are linked and appropriated within the politics of a present moment to serve the issuing party's narrative purpose.

Different factions have often employed the rhetoric of 'dawn' in association with violent circumstances. It alludes to a political awakening that manifests itself into military action, as seen above. In other instances it refers to rebirth when the political community has suffered a violent death (assassination, massacre) among its members. The commemoration of these violent deaths becomes a space to hail a major political shift whereby a disruption in the pre-existing narrative (caused by death) necessitates the emergence of a new narrative, a rebirth that mobilizes along its lines impassioned partisans struck by the tragic death.

'They sought for it to be our grave . . . it was instead our dawn'[9] is the title of a poster commemorating 13 June 1978 by the Marada movement. The movement is based in North Lebanon, and led by the Frangieh family: Suleiman Frangieh, president of Lebanon between 1970 and 1976, and his son Tony, who ran the movement's paramilitary forces. The date on the poster corresponds to the murder of the militia leader Tony Frangieh, his wife and young daughter together with a number of the Marada militiamen during an attack by the Kataeb forces on the Frangieh family residence in Ehden (fig. 3.17). Abstract modern calligraphy forms the word Lebanon, in which portraits of the victims are featured. At the composition's centre stands the Frangieh family. The overall graphic shapes and colours evoke as well the Lebanese flag. The rebirth here is the Marada's major shift in their political alliances: their break with the Lebanese Front, which they had been part of since the beginning of the war.

Diversely, a direct accusation is staged in a poster commemorating the widely condemned brutal massacre of hundreds of Palestinian civilians, on 16 September 1982, in the refugee camps of Sabra and Shatila, situated in the southern suburbs of Beirut (fig. 3.20). The violent event took place two days after the assassination of Bashir Gemayel, which resulted in the Israeli invasion of Beirut on the same day, following a long siege of the city since June. The PLO had been evacuated from Beirut in late August, under the supervision of multinational forces, as a consequence of political negotiations in the aftermath of the Israeli invasion of Lebanon. The Sabra and Shatila camps were left with civilian refugees, who fell prey to the vengeful act of members of the Lebanese Forces, undeterred by the Israeli troops who surrounded the camps. The poster features at its focal point the Star of David, in reference to the Israeli flag, enclosing the Kataeb logo. The two symbols reside at the centre of a spider web within which the civilian victims are caught – a powerful symbolic representation of the enemy's mechanism, an invisible net that catches unaware prey defenceless to the spider's deadly attack. In this poster, the link between the Kataeb and Israel, alluded to in the previous Palestinian poster, is rendered clearly visible. Here, it is not only the act of violence that is remembered, it is the perpetrator of the act, the representation of the community's belligerent enemy that gets inscribed in the collective memory.

In more brightly coloured compositions, posters commemorate significant battles that brought positive acclaim to the fighting force (figs 3.21–3.22). Zahleh, a prosperous river-valley town in the Bekaa with a majority of Christian inhabitants, suffered a severe blockade and heavy bombardment by the Syrian army in April 1981. Even though no victory was claimed, the city was later praised for its steadfastness, *Sumud Zahleh*, during the heavy assault. The LF fighters, who took up its defence and refused to surrender, were hailed as Zahleh's heroes.[10] One poster depicts the fertile landscape of the Bekaa protected by the ghostlike figure of a Virgin Mary holding a machine gun that emits a flower bouquet. The figure alludes to Zahleh's popular attribute as 'the bride of the Bekaa' but also to a monumental shrine of the Virgin Mary symbolically located in the upper hills of Zahleh. The presence of the machine gun refers to the battle, yet the deadly bullets are exchanged for peaceful flowers and the fighter is replaced by the saintly figure. The poster ignores the severity of the battle to focus instead on the image of a divine intervention that presumably saved the city.

A poster by the Shi'ite-based Amal movement features a dove forming the number six for the 6 February 1984 intifada. Amal, together with allied parties, took military control over the western sector of Beirut in 1984 following harsh battles with the Lebanese army. The army, then governed by the president and Kataeb party leader Amin Gemayel, represented the opposing camp to Amal and allied parties that staged the military uprising. The poster title 'Lift hegemony and block Zionism' refers to the Kataeb party's hegemony over the state and its alliance to Israel. The number six also refers to the mainly Shi'ite sixth brigade of the Lebanese army, who had deserted and joined Amal militiamen upon the call of Nabih Berri, Amal's political leader, depicted at the centre of the poster.[11] Beneath the figure of the leader, a crowd of people lifts some imposing barbed wire. The illustration anchored by the title connects the 6 February uprising to the resistance of Israeli occupation. In this way the commemoration extends the significance of the battle beyond a territorial conquest against a local foe to a moment of victory of the Shi'ite community over the occupying enemy.

Both posters do not depict the violence but the political esteem these battles brought to each party. Fear, violence and loss that might have resulted from these two incidents are stamped out of the memory and signs of hope and peace are remembered instead; bright colours, a dove, a mythical virgin bride, a fertile landscape, a machine gun that emits a flower bouquet are the dreamlike images associated to these events as bright memories for their respective communities.

Remembering the victory and pain of others as our own

Commemorative posters were not restricted to local events; they addressed events of regional significance that reflected the solidarity in struggle and the scope of national identification to which the community ascribed its belonging. This type of commemorative poster evoked a dominant discourse and iconography shared at a regional scale. '23 July. For the abolition of colonialism' titles a poster signed by the Socialist Arab Union. This Nasserist organization commemorates in 1977 the 1952 Egyptian revolution led by Gamal Abd-el-Nasser. It addresses the collective memory of a large audience sympathizing with the pan-Arab and reformist project that this revolution had promised (fig. 3.23). Abd-el-Nasser's portrait at the centre of a radiating sun – a vital source of life – hovers over this venerated date set in large-scale green type. Similarly, a poster by the Movement of Independent Nasserists, al-Murabitun, commemorates the union of the Egyptian and Syrian states into the United Arab Republic on 22 February 1958. The poster hails at Arab unionist sympathizers, while it makes local opponents to pan-Arabism cringe in memory of the short-lived civil war of 1958 that erupted in Lebanon in the aftermath of the union and related political conflicts. The pro-Syrian Baath organization in Lebanon commemorates the anniversary of the establishment of the Arab Socialist Baath Party on 7 April 1947 and recalls its motto 'One Arab nation with an eternal message' (fig. 3.24). The poster praises the then Syrian Baath leader and president of Syria Hafez al-Assad: 'Oh protector of the Arab people how victorious you are . . .' The poster was issued in the late 1980s, when Syrian troops had re-entered west Beirut at the request of leading local politicians to suppress the militia fighting there and reinstate order.

Solidarity with the Palestinian cause occupied a great many posters by the different factions within the Lebanese National Movement. A poster by the Syrian Social Nationalist Party (fig. 3.26) commemorates the date of the division of Palestine and the establishment of the Israeli state: 15 May 1948. The poster through the symbolic illustration clearly asserts the refusal of an American–Israeli peace plan. It shows a crossed-through white dove at the centre of the composition with the Star of David as its eye and the stars of the United States flag on its tail. The text firmly asserts the SSNP's position towards peace plans and negotiations: 'We have one policy for peace: that the enemies of this nation give it back its due rights'. Here again, as in the earlier discussed posters of the SSNP, the nation in their discourse refers to the pan-Syrian nation, which includes Palestine among the other mentioned countries of the Fertile Crescent. The poster thus does not commemorate 15 May 1948 in solidarity with the people of *another* nation, the Palestinians, but as a date that has marked the people of a pan-Syrian nation imagined as *one* community.

Conversely, 'Jerusalem Day', also known as Land Day, yearly marking the first popular uprising of Palestinians in Israel on 30 March 1976, has featured annually on many posters locally and regionally in solidarity with the Palestinian people's right to their land. Jerusalem, a central theme in Palestinian posters, has become a symbol for the Palestinian liberation struggle and was associated in many posters with the commemoration of Land Day. In *L'affiche Palestinienne: Collection Ezzedine Kalak*, the authors explain why Jerusalem became a central theme synonymous with the Palestinian struggle:

> Because Jerusalem has been historically the heart of Palestine, it got mixed with all the rhetoric of return and liberation addressed to the Palestinian and Arab masses. The importance of Jerusalem in the Palestinian media (and struggle) does not only originate from historic and national considerations; it is a major spiritual and civilization centre for people from the east and west . . . And as it holds the various religious compositions of the Arab Palestinian people, it represents an image of Palestine, the future . . . Palestine the land of coexistence where all racism, religious, ethnic and regional, withers away.[12]

Besides the idealist symbolism of Jerusalem as a cradle for coexistence across faith and ethnicity, the Dome of the Rock – a holy place of pilgrimage to the Muslim community at large, located in the old city of Jerusalem and holding exceptional architectural and aesthetic values[13] – has persisted as a reference to Jerusalem and acquired the status of a pan-Islamic symbol. Due to its wide use as a representation of Jerusalem, easily recognized for its peculiar architectural design and lavish coloured ornamentation, the icon of the Dome of the Rock has come to be directly synonymous with the city itself, acquired just like the linguistic symbols J-e-r-u-s-a-l-e-m that form the name of the city. A poster signed by the LNM features an illustration of a *fida'i* freedom fighter in full combat gear and keffiyeh, in front of him the map of Palestine with a zoom-in on a photograph of old Jerusalem focusing on the Dome of the Rock; the poster title praises 'the steadfastness of armed struggle' on the occasion of 'Jerusalem Day' (fig. 3.25).

A poster honouring 'Muslim Woman's Day' in 1984 is an example of the adaptation of the Iranian politico-religious framework and aesthetic model by Hizbullah in Lebanon (see chapter 1). 'Muslim Woman's Day' is an annual commemoration that started in Iran, upon the call of Khomeini, celebrated on the birthday of Fatima al-Zahra' – the daughter of the prophet Muhammad, also wife of Ali (the first of the Shi'ite Imams) and mother of the martyred Hassan and Hussein. As an exemplary figure of endurance and guidance as a woman in Shi'ite mythology, she provides a model for an active woman's role at times of war. The poster is divided into two parts: the image on the right side of the composition is an adapted version of a poster designed in Iran for the same purpose, whereas the left part, occupying a third of the composition, is an added Lebanese component containing the main title and the ubiquitous icon of the Dome of the Rock (fig. 3.27). Chelkowski and Dabashi, authors of *Staging a Revolution: The Art of Persuasion in the Islamic Republic of Iran*, make a good reading of the Iranian poster, which is inspired as they observe by a photograph of women in a revolutionary march:

> It contains all the characteristics of the photograph of the crowd: density, energy, equality and direction. The direction is indicated by the image of a militant woman dressed in blood-red, hovering above the marching crowd of women in their black *chador*. Her hand held high in exhortation, she seems to urge them onward . . . The outstretched fingers of the hand also stand for the five holy personalities among the Shiites. The unfurled flags in symbolic colours flying over the women add a dynamic forward thrust to the procession. On one of the green flags is written 'Oh, Zahra!' To emphasize the revolutionary spirit a rifle barrel rises from the background, behind the shoulder of the hovering image. A portrait of Ayatollah Khomeini, based on a photograph, is carried by one of the *chador*-clad women, Khomeini appears with his hand raised high as well. Another woman carries a quotation from Khomeini, written in black on the white background: 'A man ascends to heaven from his mother's lap'.[14]

The Lebanese version of the illustration includes on the bottom right another quotation, this time by Imam Mussa al-Sadr, a local Shi'ite religious figure and esteemed political leader who established the Amal movement in 1975 (see chapter 2): 'Collaboration with Israel is forbidden by God'. The marching women hold a banner upon which is inscribed *Ya Quds qadimun* ... ('Jerusalem here we come . . .'), and are directed towards the left side of the poster where the symbol of Jerusalem is placed.

Jerusalem, as a pan-Islamic symbol, is a persistent theme in the posters of Hizbullah, mostly visualized by the Dome of the Rock, denoting the struggle for Jerusalem's liberation. Hizbullah's artists acquired the icon of the Dome of the Rock through the Iranian example of imagery – posters, stamps and murals – addressing the Palestinian liberation cause as a pan-Islamic one. The colourfully drawn icon in the 'Muslim Woman's Day' poster is essentially borrowed from Iranian posters, which in turn picked the illustration from a Palestinian poster published in Beirut during the 1970s (see chapter 1).

Hizbullah places great importance on the commemoration of 'Jerusalem Day', called upon by Khomeini for all Muslims. It is observed annually on the last Friday of the month of Ramadan in a major public event meant to symbolically demonstrate the preparation for the liberation of Jerusalem. The association of 'Jerusalem Day' with the holy month of Ramadan, unlike 'Land Day', is concurrent with the call for a liberation struggle, jihad, inscribed within the fulfilment of a religious duty (see chapter 4). An early poster by Hizbullah produced in commemoration of 'Jerusalem Day' includes a quotation from Khomeini in which he calls upon every Muslim to prepare himself to confront Israel and ultimately, he claims, 'Jerusalem will return to Muslims' (fig. 3.28). The poster illustration reveals a group of four figures, two mujahidin carrying the banner of Islam, a Shi'ite cleric holding the Koran and a woman in black chador, all heading towards Jerusalem. Their destination is conveyed by the poster title *Ya Quds ... innana qadimun* ('Jerusalem . . . here we come') – a statement typically proclaimed by the gathering masses on 'Jerusalem Day'. It is emphasized by a focal image of the Dome of the Rock, towards which the group faces. The holy symbol is this time depicted walled in by the Star of David, another image found in both Iranian and Palestinian iconography, claiming Israel's offensive hold on Jerusalem.

The difference between the LNM poster and that of Hizbullah in the commemoration of 'Jerusalem Day' is not just a matter of dates (30 March vs last Friday of Ramadan), nor only a secular versus a religiously inscribed struggle of liberation (*fida'i* vs *mujahid*). It also lies in the representation of the imagined place of Jerusalem. The former locates Jerusalem at the heart of a map of the Palestinian nation with defined geopolitical boundaries. The other represents Jerusalem as a holy place that belongs to the *Umma* (Muslim community/nation) at large, as part of an imagined continuous landscape, where boundaries are obstacles artificially imposed by foreign entities but that can be surmounted. The jail-like walls in the shape of the Star of

David surrounding the Dome of the Rock and the barbed wire, referring to the southern Lebanese border, are forced, the illustration suggests, by the three nations whose flags are represented: France, the USA and Israel. The commemoration of 'Jerusalem Day' in Hizbullah's poster is not only in solidarity with the dispossessed Palestinian people, as with the LNM. Above all, it summons up the struggle of a Muslim *Umma* deprived of its holy site, remembering the pain as 'our own'.

4

Martyrdom

The great wars of this century are extraordinary not so much in the unprecedented scale on which they permitted people to kill, as in the colossal numbers persuaded to lay down their lives.[1]

The martyr, an age-old term for the one who is killed for his/her beliefs, has had its share of sanctification in the history of struggles; the most noble of all heroes is thought to be the person who dies fighting in defence of these beliefs, be they religious, national or ideological. The universal language of martyrdom is laden with emotional themes of courage, self-sacrifice, nobility, purity and righteousness. While glorified martyrs have mostly been historical leaders, the posters that will be discussed in this chapter praise more or less ordinary partisans fallen during the course of the war. Unlike the previously addressed model of the mythical leader, whose path can be followed yet his role remains supreme, the heroic model of the martyred combatant is an accessible reality to the members of the community.

Martyrdom is another widespread theme characterizing the subject matter of a large number of posters. The civil war in Lebanon witnessed several warring factions or fronts at its different stages. Each front was composed of diverse parties and distinct military movements that fought on one side. Political parties competed in declaring their share of zealous fighting by proclaiming the amount of martyrs they had 'offered' up to the common cause of the front. The number of fallen heroes becomes an indicator of a party's share of participation on a front and a proof of its commitment and sacrifice in the defence of an existential cause. Martyrs are hence attributed a great deal of importance within parties and factions. The party honours its martyrs with the nobility of a cause just as it is glorified through the number of martyrs fallen in its name.

In their most basic function, martyrdom posters act as public obituaries. It is common practice in Lebanon to post obituaries in public spaces, primarily around where the deceased lived and worked, to inform neighbours and acquaintances of the death, condolences, and funeral proceedings. As a continuation of this practice, the martyr poster is issued by a political party acting as the 'family' of the deceased, to inform their community about the loss of one of its members and to honour them as a martyr. The posters are displayed within the deceased's family's neighbourhood and in and around the military locales of the party to which he/she belonged.

It is hard for a youth impassioned by the same cause to pass by these posters without being affected and probably, if only for a brief moment, imagining him/herself in the photograph with his/her name praised as the martyr hero. In fact, one designer for a party went as far as designing a fictive martyr poster for himself. On several occasions, the immediate family of a martyr has asked the party's media office for posters to be made to honour their loved one as a hero, sometimes going so far as specifying the design of the poster to be 'like the one designed for the martyr of such and such family'. Consequently, even at their basic informative level these posters acquire a different purpose: that of recruiting potential fighters, encouraged by the 'noble' example of their friend, neighbour, relative and comrade.

Although the visual rhetoric may vary greatly, there are common codes that characterize this thematic typology of posters: a portrait of the martyr accompanied by the name, date, and sometimes location or battlefield where the combatant fought and died. The designs of the martyr posters range from a standardized obituary format to very complex representations of martyrdom combined with rich visual and textual rhetoric specific to the party. The visual representation varies depending on the position of the deceased within the party hierarchy, how he or she died and on the significance of the battle in which he or she fought. The posters also vary depending on the party's discourse on the concept of martyrdom, whether from within a secular or religious framework.

The poignant character of these posters is hard to avoid, even today, considering the distance of time and discursive framework that could separate a viewer from such posters. The martyr posters attest to the deaths that the war has brutally left us. Borrowing Benedict Anderson's words, these posters confront us with 'the colossal numbers [of people] persuaded to lay down their lives'. Each poster repeatedly asserts the death of a person: you see the face, read the name, dates of birth and passing. The martyr posters are striking in their immediacy. While the other theme posters might be compelling in their idealized political rhetoric of noble causes, heroic endeavours and mythical leaders, the martyr posters proclaim that these narratives were very real to those who died in their cause.

The obituary format

The most common martyr poster, which has become a classical type across all parties and factions, is the one that follows the basic principles of an obituary. To start with, the poster features a photograph of the deceased, most commonly a passport or identity-card photograph, the one that is readily available to the party or from the martyr's family. In fact some of these photographs picture the deceased at a much younger age, while the 'luckier' ones happen to have a more recent photograph, sometimes in a virile pose of a fearless combatant in arms. In many cases the same photograph was also used in the obituary section of a local newspaper. The photograph is coupled with the name and a short combatant biography: date and place of birth, date of adherence to the party, date of participation in the specific front, the date and battle in which he/she has fallen – 'martyred in the battles of the Northern Matn, on 11-5-1980, in defence of Lebanon's unity and its [greater] national belonging'. The name is typically accompanied by praise, which can vary from the standard 'the martyr hero' to more romanticized and elaborate statements such as 'The party takes pride in you as a hero and the land cherishes you as a martyr'. Another level of information is reserved to the party proclaiming its martyr – 'Amal movement . . . presents to its pious audience, the martyr . . .', usually accompanied by the party's logo. In many cases, party and front announce their martyrs, affirming the active participation of the party on a particular battlefront – 'The martyr of the Lebanese National Resistance Front, the martyr of the Lebanese Communist Party'. All this information is laid out in a basic template design that gets reproduced for the different martyrs; a by-product of modern means of mass production, this system economizes on time and creates a standardized visual identity, whereby with recurrent use the poster becomes an immediate marker of the party concerned.

Collective martyrs

Besides the individualized format of martyr posters, parties also proclaim their martyrs in collective form through a single poster. Such posters combine a number of martyrs who have fallen over a period of time on a specific battlefront, or on the same date in a major battle or significant communal commando operation. These posters glorify the party inasmuch as they praise martyrs as a collective. Posters are filled with the portraits and names of martyrs: their collectivity creates the visual message of the poster. 'A constellation/squadron of martyrs of the Islamic Resistance' is the title for one such poster (fig. 4.19). Another by the LCP states, 'From the Mina [northern port city in Tripoli] to the nation, 1924–1986' (fig. 4.20). Yet another by the SSNP (fig. 4.21) celebrates its 54th anniversary, in 1986, while remembering its 'heroic martyrs who fell in the battle of national pride in the northern Matn'. It is mostly in such typology of martyr posters that the party's 'commitment' and 'self-sacrifice' for the cause is substantiated by the overwhelming number of martyrs fallen in its name.

Instead of just a host of martyr portraits, other posters add another level of meaning visually by employing symbolic imagery that further unifies the collectivity of martyrs and inscribes it within the discourse of the party concerned. Two such interesting examples are posters by the LCP and the Kataeb, both produced in 1976, in the early phase of Lebanon's war.

'Martyrs of the Lebanese Communist Party, March 1975–March 1976; martyrs in the battle against the fascist isolationist plan in defence of Lebanon, its unity, Arab identity and in defence of the Palestinian resistance' (fig. 4.22). This large poster by the LCP lists the names of martyrs and where each fought and died, enclosed in red Communist stars; the stars are spread across the map of Lebanon, which in turn acts as the macro-container of the Communist martyrs. The poster's cause, suggested in the title, is concurrent with the broad lines of the LNM, the front in which the LCP took active part. By this poster the LCP declares its share of active participation in that front in the two-year war of 1975–6. The graphic image also implies that the LCP adherents are not geographically circumscribed but have actually engaged on all fronts across the whole of Lebanon and 'defended its unity'.

On the other hand, the poster by the Kataeb pays tribute to its own martyrs who have 'died for Lebanon to live' (fig. 4.23). By doing so the poster equally romanticizes the Kataeb's patriotism, the loss of its members for the continuity of the cause, and reaffirms their pledge as the defenders of Lebanon (see chapter 3), which, in the Kataeb's outlook, is threatened by Communism, Arabism and 'foreign' armed forces, specifically the Palestinian resistance at the time. It is that same outlook which is referred to in the above-discussed LCP poster as 'fascist isolationist'. The names of the martyrs and the dates of their passing figure into the Kataeb party's logo: a graphic abstraction of the cedar tree, the central symbol on the Lebanese flag. The eight trees are laid out to collectively form yet another Kataeb tree, set out on a red background evoking blood and sacrifice. The graphic imagery (red star, cedar tree, map) in such posters has a double function: first its own symbolic meaning, and second it acts as a container to the names of martyrs individually and in their totality, unifying the collective martyrs within the symbols of the party.

Another type of collective martyr posters features a central image as the main message of the poster accompanied by photographic portraits of the martyrs and anchored by a lyrical title. The visual statement, mostly romanticized in content, affixes the martyrdom of the party members in the larger cause suggested by the image and title. In a surreal desertlike landscape, rifles, planted in the land like tombstones, mark the burial of the deceased combatants (fig. 4.24). The illustration suggests that the martyrs in the photographs have fallen but the spirit of armed struggle persists above the ground in which they have been buried. It is a land to which they are firmly bound – 'The land is ours' – and in whose cause they have offered their lives – 'The martyrs of defiance to occupation in defence of the nation's land'. A hand holds tightly on to one of the rifles, an indication of life in an arid landscape; for what appear to be like tombstones show themselves to be a 'defiant' life born out of the land from the seeds of martyrdom. In an equally hopeful and idyllic image, another poster praises the 'high-quality operation', in the southern Lebanon mountain Toumat Niha under Israeli occupation in 1987, as much as it pays tribute to the martyrs who have fallen in that operation (fig. 4.25). The image connotes that their martyrdom has brought back life to an occupied land; the sun rises from behind a black mountain landscape and shines over blossoming flowers.

Acclaimed martyr-heroes

A further variation on the martyr poster is the one dedicated to a noted member of the party. Besides the posters of major leader martyrs (see chapter 2), others pay homage to esteemed, high-ranking members as noted martyrs; still others commemorate 'heroic' combatants whose martyrdom played a significant politico-military role in the party history. These posters feature the deceased's portrait as the central subject, yet do not adopt the standardized format of the obituary. Each is conceived to portray the individual character of the subject and inscribes his/her martyrdom in the narrative of the party. Unlike the common use of passport photos, more artistic efforts and symbolic values are put into the martyr's portrait and a visual narrative that surrounds it.

'The martyred leader Ahmad al-Meer al-Ayoubi (Abu Hassan), member of the political bureau of the Lebanese Communist Party'. The portrait of al-Ayoubi is stylized in the manner of 1970s Cuban posters: a minimum of shapes and lines define the face, tonal variations of the same colour form the shaded areas and highlight one side. In its iconography, the poster equally shares the international symbolism of the red rose for Communist parties in general. The red flower broken by a bullet here poetically refers to the pain or damage that the party has endured in losing an esteemed member (fig. 4.26).

Likewise, Sheikh Ragheb Harb, assassinated in 1984 by Israeli agents, gets his share of veneration by the Shi'ite political community; both Amal and Hizbullah have produced a number of posters to commemorate the Sheikh's martyrdom (figs 4.35–4.36). Harb was a prominent member of the Association of the Ulama of Jabal Amel, a militant organization of local Shi'ite clergy with ideological ties to Iran. Harb planned and carried out resistance operations against Israeli occupation, thus contributing to the establishment and extension of Hizbullah in the south of Lebanon.[2] His portrait, a recognized icon to this day, appears amidst a rich visual narrative, replete with codes ingrained in a politico-religious Shi'ite iconography pertaining to struggle and martyrdom. The signs and meanings of this particular iconography will be discussed in detail on pages 130–4.

Beginning in 1982, several parties participated in the resistance to Israeli occupation. The Lebanese National Resistance Front, a coalition of leftist and nationalist parties, was formed in the aftermath of the Israeli invasion, calling for a popular resistance of the occupation. In this front more than others, the parties outbid each other in proclaiming their share of 'self-sacrifice' in the 'noble national cause' of resisting occupation and heroic confrontation of the enemy. Posters for martyrs of the resistance were many, among them some that venerated martyrs of a 'heroic operation', especially when it was the first of its kind within military resistance in Lebanon. The commemoration of such 'first-kind' military operations saluted both martyr and party as landmarks of national resistance. Such martyr posters also had custom-made designs that set them apart in significance from the standard obituary format.

A poster by the Lebanese National Resistance Front commemorates Khaled Alwan, a member of the Syrian Social Nationalist Party, as the first to engage in an armed confrontation with Israeli soldiers in Beirut (fig. 4.29). Although Alwan died two years later, not in this operation, the SSNP chose to remember him as the 'hero of the Wimpy operation'. On 24 September 1982, ten days after the Israeli invasion of Beirut, Khaled Alwan opened fire on a group of three Israeli soldiers who were sitting at a table in the Wimpy café in Hamra Street, a central location in west Beirut. An Israeli commander died and another was wounded. Alwan's action was followed by a series of resistance operations, which led the Israeli army to withdraw from Beirut by the end of September. The portrait of Alwan overlaps a photograph of the café, where Israeli soldiers had gathered following the incident. The photograph is framed as in a postcard, with a text, cutting diagonally across its corner, quoting a message spread by the Israeli army while withdrawing from Beirut: 'Do not fire, we are leaving'. Thus a national historic moment is cited to substantiate the accomplishment of the resistance and particularly that of Alwan. The upper-left corner of the poster bears one of the logos of the Lebanese National Resistance Front. This variation was created by the Syrian Social Nationalist Party to identify its resistance operations and its own martyr posters. The design features a red calligraphic inscription of the front's name that forms a cedar tree enclosed within a circle; beneath the tree is written 'until liberation and victory'.

The Lebanese Communist Party had its own logo variant, but it was hardly used on their posters. It is composed of a red dove that encloses a cedar tree, forming the colours and symbols of the Lebanese flag. The logo is intercepted in its centre by an upright rifle, symbolizing armed resistance, and topped by the red Communist star on its right corner. Unlike their opponents – the Kataeb and Lebanese Forces – whose iconography relies on the Lebanese state symbols (see chapter 2), the SSNP and LCP do not normally use these symbols in their poster iconography. In this particular logo they resort to these symbols to assert the patriotic endeavour in the resistance to occupation.

The resistance to Israeli occupation in the south took on a new form of commando operations against the occupying Israeli army. 'Martyrdom operations', referred to in Western media nowadays as 'suicide bombing', were carried out by militants of both genders and coordinated by secular as well as religious armed factions. Acclaimed and commemorated in posters and elsewhere as the bravest and purest of martyrs by their respective parties, the names of these young men and women still echo in the minds of partisans of the resistance. The controversial subject of 'martyrdom operations' or 'suicide bombing' – which was brutally amplified and took on new meanings after the Palestinian intifada, 11 September and the unsettled situation in Iraq – is not the subject of our discussion here. Just to frame the posters dedicated to martyrs of such operations, it will suffice us to say that in the Lebanese case, 'martyrdom operations' were viewed by their authors and coordinators as legitimate means of resistance when under occupation, with extremely limited military options against the powerful apparatus of the Israeli army. These extreme methods were met with divided positions among the Lebanese population. On one hand some hailed these as legendary martyrs, the ultimate heroes in the noble cause of defending their land and people, while others cringed at the unfathomable thought of how young men and women could give up their lives so willingly and in such a horrifying manner. Speaking of his sister Loula Abboud, a combatant in the Lebanese Communist Party who died at the age of 19 exploding herself against Israeli soldiers in her home town (see fig. 4.12), Dr Fouad Elias Abboud explained: 'All cases of martyrdom are cases of fighting for your existence . . . The freedom fighter chooses death as a final choice. He doesn't choose it from the beginning. It's after he can not fight anymore that he decides to kill himself. And she was fighting the Israelis within her own village. She was not fighting Israelis in Israel.'[3]

The Islamic Resistance, the military arm of Hizbullah, marked in a poster, produced in 1984, the second annual commemoration of the martyr Ahmad Kassir by proclaiming him 'The first in the reign of heroism, the pioneer of martyrdom operations' (fig. 4.27, and see also fig. 1.32). The bombing destroyed the Israeli headquarters in Tyre, South Lebanon, on 11 November 1982 and took the lives of around 100 members of the Israeli army. In the poster's intricate photomontage composition, Kassir's portrait hovers on top of a photograph of the destroyed site. His bust is framed by a bright shimmering halo, just like a divine figure. Hizbullah issued this poster with the party's official establishment in 1984 and proclaimed Kassir's operation as its own. With the commemoration of Kassir, Hizbullah asserts that it had active cells as of 1982 and declares *its own* martyr to be the first among the 'martyrdom operations'. Hizbullah issued several posters in the following years commemorating Ahmad Kassir on 11 November. The date in fact got annually institutionalized as Martyr's Day in the party's calendar of symbolic public commemorations.

A poster announcing 'The week of the resistant woman' in the first annual commemoration of the martyrdom of Sana' Mehaidli shows her portrait in the foreground at the lead of other women martyrs; the poster features her as a role model for women's active participation in the war front. Mehaidli, a combatant in the SSNP, was the first woman to lead a 'martyrdom operation', in April 1985. The soft strokes of the illustration and the overall feminine and romantic expression of the poster contrast with the violence of her death (fig. 4.30). The call for an active women's role in resistance is progressive in a patriarchal society consumed by traditional gender roles, yet the visual representation in this poster does not match that challenge. It remains quite conservative and does not break from the typical stereotype of romanticized femininity. Perhaps it is intentionally designed in that manner to reflect the idea that women can be as active as men on the war front without totally compromising their 'femininity'.

Another young and memorable face is that of Bilal Fahs, designated 'the groom of the south' as he was supposed to get married a week later; a poster portrays him youthful and smiling. Beneath his portrait, a comic-book-style illustration paradoxically narrates the brutality of the event. He drove a Mercedes car, loaded with explosives, into an Israeli army position in the south of Lebanon. The explosion, an orange 'bang' at the centre of the poster, shatters the symbol of the state of Israel (fig. 4.28).

'Martyrdom operation' posters: the case of the SSNP

In 1985 the Syrian Social Nationalist Party initiated a new kind of poster series dedicated to the authors of 'martyrdom operations'. These martyr posters were visually unified by a standardized design system, yet did not conform to the typical components of the obituary poster. The poster was in fact prepared before the military operation took place: in other words, a martyr's poster was in the making before his/her martyrdom.

'Martyrdom operations' took months of preparation in which the combatant gets ready in terms of military tactics and also psychologically, explains a member of the SSNP.[4] Towards the end when the combatant is ready to go on his mission, he/she is filmed giving a farewell message to his/her comrades in resistance and parents, in which he/she explains the reasons behind such a drastic choice and the political meaning his/her martyrdom could carry to the cause of resistance and liberation of South Lebanon. A short video is produced from the footage and distributed outside the confines of the party.[5] The promotional phenomenon brought by these video statements goes beyond the scope of our study here, but they are relevant in view of the fact that the SSNP posters were based on excerpts from these statements and photographs taken during filming.

That poignant aspect brings an unprecedented immediacy to the poster: the viewer is confronted with the last photograph and words of a young man or woman about to give their life, knowing, by the mere fact of the poster's having been published, that the person has passed away. While other posters focus on one moment that is the date of martyrdom/death, these create an uneasy restlessness between two moments. We see in the poster a moment of life, anticipating death, as the person addresses a possible viewer, in words and through the camera. We don't see (or read) the other moment of death, their imminent martyrdom, but it is referred to by their words and confirmed by the existence of the poster. The tension created by those two moments, anticipating death and death, simultaneously present in the poster is difficult to resolve for the viewer, and renders these posters quite unique in their representation of the difficulty of the subject.

The poster consists of only three graphic components: at the top is the logo of the Lebanese National Resistance Front (the SSNP's variation discussed above); a large photograph of the martyr occupies the centre of the poster; beneath it figures a statement from the martyr's message followed by his/her name. The statements chosen for these posters address in different ways the resistance to occupation and the choice of armed struggle in confronting the enemy:

'The Israeli enemy is the enemy of my nation and we will not let it rest – Wajdi'

'With the arms of will, determination and resistance we shall be victorious – Maryam'

The pose and setting in the photographs are as studied as the statements uttered: combatants in military attire raise their arms in a salute, behind them the flag and logo of the SSNP, and a tribute to the idealized martyr *za'im*, the founder Antun Saadeh, is also present in the backdrop through some of his famous quotes or a framed portrait photo (figs 4.31–4.33). While the text attests to the martyr's commitment to the cause of national resistance, the photograph confirms his/her loyalty to the party and its symbols: flag, emblem and founder.

In one of these posters, the photograph breaks from the directed pose and setting (fig. 4.34). It shows the martyr sitting facing the camera, his firm gaze confronting the viewer. Behind him is a wall onto which posters of previous SSNP martyrs have been posted, similar in photographic setting to the ones discussed above (we see among these the bottom part of 4.33). He also wears a T-shirt whose top part is visible and includes the statement 'The symbol of national Lebanese resistance' crowning the top of a head. We don't get to see the face but we understand that it's yet another martyr for whom T-shirts have been dedicated in his memory. The setting projects an imagined *mise en abîme* illusory game, whereby the poster containing the photograph of the martyr against a background of previous martyr posters will be put on a wall behind another martyr to come, whose poster in turn will be placed behind another . . . ad infinitum – a seemingly endless repetition of martyr posters inside a martyr poster. The setting in this particular photograph, unlike the previous ones, does not only allude to the party's symbols, but to the collectivity of martyrs the party has sacrificed for the cause of resistance.

Jihad and martyrdom in the Islamic Resistance posters

Martyr posters of the Islamic Resistance, the military wing of Hizbullah, are replete with signs specific to martyrdom inscribed within a Shi'ite politico-religious heritage. The particularity of this iconography forms a typology of martyr posters that necessitates a focused study.

Hizbullah's military resistance to Israeli occupation is not only framed within a national cause as seen in previous cases but also deeply rooted in the fulfilment of a religious legal obligation, *wajib shar'i*, to wage a jihad[6] – to strive in the cause of God against oppressors of the *Umma* (Muslim community). Hizbullah conceive of their military role through the Islamic Resistance as a 'defensive jihad' against oppression; Sheikh Naim Qassem, a founding member of Hizbullah, writes in *Hizbullah: The Story from Within*, 'It is the defence by Muslims of their land, their people or their own selves upon facing aggression or occupation. This is not only considered legitimate, but a [religious] duty.'[7]

Central to jihad is the notion of martyrdom or more precisely 'readiness for martyrdom' in Hizbullah's discourse; the desire to strive righteously is concurrent with the willingness to sacrifice one's life and material belongings for a holy cause. Jihad and its mujahidin, those who strive in the cause of God, are accorded a high status in Islam; it is believed that the mujahidin will be rewarded in the afterlife in return for their sacrifice.[8] Hizbullah ascribes unprecedented value to the culture of martyrdom and to the religious conception of a better life after death.[9] This is surely evident in the martyr posters of Hizbullah, where verses from the Koran pertaining to paradise and the afterlife are a recurrent theme:

'God has bought from the believers their lives and their wealth for paradise will be theirs as they fight in God's path.'

'But do not think of those that have been slain in God's cause as dead. Nay, they are alive!'

'And those who have strived in our name we shall offer them our means.'

The posters sanctify as much as they venerate the martyrdom of the mujahidin by continuously emphasizing the 'Islamic' character of the resistance. Hizbullah's martyr posters persistently feature the icon of the Dome of the Rock[10] in reference to Jerusalem, the third holy city to the Muslim community after Mecca and Medina, both in Saudi Arabia (figs 1.31 and 4.39–4.40). The icon has become a pan-Islamic sacred symbol, widely used by different factions in the region to denote the struggle for the liberation of Jerusalem. Hizbullah attaches a great deal of importance to the liberation of Jerusalem as a pan-Islamic cause in its posters in general, particularly those produced for the commemorative event of 'Jerusalem Day' discussed earlier in chapter 3. This symbol's prominence in martyr posters in particular, all the more in posters devoted for martyrs fallen on Lebanese territories, attests to Hizbullah's conception of resistance to Israeli occupation in Lebanon as tied to a larger pan-Islamic struggle.

One of the Islamic Resistance martyr posters designates Jerusalem as the kiblah (direction of prayer for Muslims) in lieu of Mecca.[11] It features the lying body of a mujahid wrapped in a white burial shroud; his body is seen in perspective through the depth of a mihrab (prayer niche), both body and mihrab directed towards Jerusalem instead of, as normally, towards Mecca. The resistance names its member, fallen in the Bekaa in 1985, 'the martyr of Islam'. The poster thus claims Jerusalem as the kiblah of the mujahidin, its liberation the ultimate jihad (fig. 4.39).

The overwhelming visual and textual rhetoric present in the posters asserts not only a prevailing Islamic character but a particularly Shi'ite dominant discourse on martyrdom and jihad, exemplified by Imam al-Hussein's dissent from the Umayyad rule and his subsequent martyrdom in Karbala in the year 680.[12] The seminal event of Karbala, narrated and commemorated yearly through collective acts of remembrance during the first ten days of the month of Muharram, culminating in public communal rituals in the Ashura processions on the tenth, has deeply embedded in the Shi'ite collective consciousness a whole repertory of symbols laden with Shi'ite politico-religious meaning pertaining to oppression, struggle and martyrdom. The internalized repertory of signs in Ashura commemoration, 'read and reread into the changing reality of the communal anxieties',[13] has changed the conception of death and defeat and converted submission and passivity to agency.[14]

Naim Qassem clearly articulates the party's reliance on a strong model of martyrdom such as that of Imam Hussein:

> A society nurtured with the exemplary story of Imam al-Hussein and his followers is enriched and reinforced by their conduct. . . . We have learned through Imam al-Hussein that the love of martyrdom is part of the love of God. We have learned to glorify jihad for the sake of Islam. Generations after al-Hussein's resurgence in Karbala, we still learn from the magnificent accomplishments that materialized through his martyrdom. His vision was not momentary or restricted to the battle: it was directed at the future of Islam and of the Muslims.[15]

The appeal of the sacred memory of Imam Hussein's martyrdom and its interpretive power in current struggle was not restricted to Lebanon's Shi'ite community; it had already been effectively put into use by Khomeini in Iran for the purpose of the revolution and the later Iran–Iraq war.[16] In Khomeini's words:

> It is said of the Prince of World Martyrs that the more his noble companions were killed and the closer he got to high noon of Ashura, the more his most gracious complexion became excited, his happiness intensified. With every martyr he offered, he got one step closer to victory. The aim is [one's] conviction, to struggle for it, and revolutionary victory, not life, and in this world not all the despicable distractions of it.[17]

Influenced by the Iranian method and iconography (see chapter 1), Hizbullah has transposed the model of Imam Hussein's exemplary jihad and martyrdom into a dominant narrative that constitutes most of the Islamic Resistance martyr posters. This narrative is articulated by the repertory of signs and iconic heritage that had been institutionalized and sustained through Ashura commemoration.

Blood is an overwhelming protagonist in the narrative of martyrdom, referring to self-sacrifice. It is portrayed in a grotesque exuberance, a literal visual expression of a bloodbath (figs 1.31 and 4.35–4.37). One such poster depicts a succession of fists emerging out of a sea of blood, firmly holding banners of testimonial to Islam; the image provides a visualization of 'jihad for the sake of Islam'. The image is anchored by the statement: 'The blood of martyrs is the most honest expression of blood vanquishing the sword'. The text is adapted from the words of Khomeini claiming that 'in Karbala blood has vanquished the sword', implying that the historical martyrdom of al-Hussein (blood) has brought accomplishments to Islam and has overcome the lethal power of the oppressive enemy (the sword). The poster thus creates a parallel between the martyrdom of al-Hussein and that of the Islamic Resistance mujahidin; for their blood too is sacrificed for the sake of 'a better future of Islam' and has kept Islam's banner up against the enemy's overpowering military apparatus (fig. 4.37).

In the same way that the fist, a familiar image of dissent, is coupled with blood, so too is the AK-47-type rifle. In such cases dissent is taken to its ultimate measure, that of armed struggle, as with other liberation and revolutionary movements of the seventies; the Kalashnikov is the icon of resistance. Yet these icons of secular leftist origins are articulated here with Islamic references and particularly Shi'ite codes of jihad and martyrdom, affirming yet again the sanctity of the resistance not only as a national cause but foremost as a religious commitment.

One of the posters commemorating the martyrdom of Sheikh Ragheb Harb (see page 126) visually illustrates Hizbullah's idiom that peace can only be achieved through armed struggle and martyrdom (fig. 4.36).[18] A 'sea of blood' creates through its inverse form the figure of a dove, symbol of peace; blood and dove are tightly integrated so as to create a symbiotic positive-and-negative formal relationship of two opposite forces forming a whole. From the blood emerges the tip of a rifle coupled with a red tulip, a symbol largely used in Iranian revolutionary iconography signifying martyrdom.

'Our glory . . . our pride and the Prince of Martyrs . . . the guide to our path': with this title a poster proclaims collectively nine martyrs of the Islamic Resistance. Its image shows nine silhouettes of mujahidin marching victoriously, holding up their rifles in a manner similar to depictions of left-wing revolutionary guerrillas. However, the banner of Islam raised at the front of the line along with the red band that adorns the heads of the silhouetted men distinguish the fighters from other, secular liberation movements and identify them as mujahidin, freedom fighters of an *Islamic* resistance movement (fig. 4.38). The headband, usually marked with political and religious short statements or invocations, is believed to have been worn by Imam Hussein in the battle of Karbala, and was subsequently adopted into the Ashura repertory of symbols. It found its way into the attire of Hizbullah's combatants by way of the Iranian model.[19] Posters often depict the martyred combatants as heroic mujahidin adorned with such headbands, following yet again the supreme example of their 'Prince of Martyrs' (figs 4.39–4.41).

5

Belonging

In the field of collective identities, we are always dealing with the creation of a 'we' which can only exist by the demarcation of a 'they'.[1]

In situations of warfare, when diplomacy collapses in face of armed confrontation, the opposition between a collective 'we' and 'they' is amplified into an antagonistic relation of enmity. Chantal Mouffe writes in *On the Political* that the antagonistic relation of friend/enemy occurs when the 'they' is perceived as contesting the identity of the 'we' and as threatening its existence and well-being.[2] The identification and demarcation of a 'they' as the hostile enemy becomes essential in constructing and securing a consensual 'we'. The antagonism in the portrayal of the self versus enemy is thus central to the construction of collective imaginaries. Posters, among other means of dissemination of political discourse, have served in normalizing a friend-versus-enemy antagonism. Images of the enemy are created and opposed to those of an imagined self. The image of the enemy as a monstrous and threatening entity, in the history of modern political posters, is a recurrent theme calling for emotional responses involving hate, fear and paranoia of the other.

In an essay examining the phenomenon of graphic hate in modern political propaganda Steven Heller notes that 'the process of demonic manufacture, wherein the object of abhorrence must be thoroughly stripped of its human characteristics, is essential in securing mass hostility towards one group or another'.[3] Dehumanized images of the enemy in political posters concretize the object of enmity through symbolic means of representation, thereby naturalizing the constructed hostile traits as intrinsic attributes of the enemy/other.

> In the beginning we create the enemy. Before the weapon comes the image. We think others to death and then invent the battle-axe or the ballistic missiles with which to actually kill them. Propaganda precedes technology.[4]

In his book *Faces of the Enemy: Reflections of the Hostile Imagination*, Sam Keen examines how the image of the enemy is manufactured in the history of political propaganda and argues that the 'hostile imagination' justifies and legitimizes hostile acts. He claims that throughout history the 'hostile imagination' has relied on a standard set of signs by which the enemy is represented as a dehumanized other. Keen outlines archetypal images of the enemy, namely: the enemy as stranger, aggressor, faceless, enemy of God, barbarian, beastlike and as death itself.

Among the political posters of wartime Lebanon emerges the polarity of a 'we vs they' representation; an imagined righteous 'self' is set against an image of the enemy as a hostile 'other'. Many of the archetypes presented by Keen apply in the Lebanese case; the stereotypes of a dehumanized enemy are evident. The posters in this chapter reveal the internal antagonism between political communities as it unfolded through the different war phases and fronts. They also show the communities' various relations to regional threats, and conversely their belonging to greater nationalist frameworks. Each local camp's articulation of the symbols of hostility and communal struggle is at odds with the others'. Mouffe maintains that political identities are not intrinsic: 'the constitution of a specific "we" always depends on the type of "they" from which it is differentiated'. The *types* of enemies drawn in Lebanon's wartime posters served in the constitution of collective imaginaries around the self. However, these self-representations were not fixed but rather varied with the formations and transformations of political identities throughout the war period, as they were symptomatic of the shifting political struggles and battles over territory.

Unlike in other theme posters addressed in the previous chapters – leadership, commemoration and martyrdom – the graphic representation here is not restricted to ideological or lyrical political rhetoric. It extends to direct physical and military power, often offensive and violent. These posters are specific to an intense warfare climate, in which the objective is to secure consensus within each community by reinforcing discourses of communal threat, resistance and belonging. It is worth noting that the fighters featured on these posters are not represented in portraits of specific people, as seen in the posters of heroic leaders and martyrs. They are represented instead through generic figures of heroes, with which members of a particular community could identify; likewise '"The" enemy is always singular', observes Keen.[5] We could claim that the subject of representation, for the 'we' and 'they', is the collective condensed and distilled into a common icon where all distinctions and diversities are diluted, hence the profusion of stereotypes acting as conventional codes for immediate signification.

Identifying the enemy

Derogatory representations of the enemy in traditional attire have been employed to reinforce the opponent's otherness at the level of ethnicity and to present it as belonging to a backward and undeveloped community. In one such poster, 'The Arab barbaric tribes' is inscribed on a banner drawn beneath a chaotic mass of an antlike army being crushed by two gigantic feet (fig. 5.13). Another poster shows troops entering Lebanon, with the title 'Your tricks are uncovered and justice will prevail'. They are portrayed satirically, coming out of a large wooden horse's belly, pulling camels and wearing djellabas – traditional Arab attire. Through allegory, referring to the military ploy of the Trojan horse, the image tells us that the soldiers have entered Lebanon treacherously (fig. 5.1).

Both posters allude to the Arab Deterrent Force, which was dispatched to Lebanon in November 1976 in accordance with the ceasefire called by a summit meeting of the Arab States. The ADF consisted of peacekeeping troops from Syria, Sudan, Yemen and Saudi Arabia. While the non-Syrian ADF troops left Lebanon in 1979, the Syrians who formed the majority remained in force under the guise of 'peacekeeping'. Although the Syrian troops were welcomed by the Lebanese Front in 1976 – their intervention prevented a possible victory by the Palestinian forces and allied Lebanese National Movement – their continued military control was contested by that same front in 1978. By that year, Syria's network of alliance with the warring camps in Lebanon had shifted. Following the assassination of Kamal Jumblatt in 1977, the LNM led by Walid Jumblatt had begun to forge reconciliation with Syria. The Israeli invasion of South Lebanon in 1978 and Israel's military support of and alliance with the Lebanese Front parties precipitated the conflict between Syria and those parties. In the same year, Syrian troops entered into intense armed confrontation with the Lebanese Front militias. The battle, known as the '100 days' war', resulted in heavy Syrian artillery pounding of east Beirut towns of mainly Christian constituency that represented the stronghold of the LF militias.

These two posters were not signed by any party, yet it is clear that they were published by factions belonging to the Lebanese Front. That can be inferred from the towns featured on them as victims of the aggression: Ain el-Rummaneh, Ashrafieh, Furn el-Shubbak, towns that were targets of heavy Syrian assaults in 1978. The authors of these posters affirm their belonging to a modern Lebanese national community that is distinct from its neighbouring Arab ones. The latter are portrayed as inferior, undeveloped and consumed by traditions (djellabas and camels); a deceit-ful neighbour who employs archaic means (the Trojan horse) to conquer and violate Lebanese sovereignty and threatens particularly the well-being of the Christian community. Such portrayal is requisite to the hegemonic formation of a collective self-consciousness among the Lebanese Christian community that imagines itself and its 'Lebaneseness' in opposition to all the enemy's above-mentioned traits – as an advanced and civilized modern culture distinct from an 'Arab barbaric tribal' community.

The question of a Lebanese identity distinguished from an Arab one has long preoccupied the discourse of right-wing Christian political communities. The rise of regional Arab unionist parties in the 1950s intensified the discourse of a threat-ened Lebanese identity and Christian minority within what was perceived as an overwhelmingly Arab/Muslim region. The political struggle that led to the civil war further tightened the articulation between a nationalist identity (Lebanese) and a confessional one (Christian) within the discourse of the Lebanese Front coalition. A number of posters issued by members of that front reveal the demarcation of a hostile other characterized as inferior and barbaric versus an advanced and modern image of the self. This self-representation coincides with an overbearing colonial outlook, long experienced in the region, of a Western self set against the image of the colonized.

This is even further articulated in a representation of an internal Lebanese op-ponent to the Lebanese Front. In this case the line is drawn at the Front's confes-sional belonging. A photograph shows a Druze in his traditional mountain attire, captured in a moment of total frenzy, holding a knife out in a threatening gesture; the title above the photograph reads al-qatil ('the murderer'). In the same poster, a facing text/image couple forms a contrary message: a fighter dressed in his full modern combat gear kneels before a crucifix, and below the photograph is written al-muqatil ('the combatant') (fig. 5.2). The poster was published in 1983 at a moment of fierce confrontation in the mountains between the Lebanese Forces, including the Kataeb, and the militias of the Progressive Socialist Party, each camp claim-ing protection over its respective confessional community belonging. The unruly violence that shook the mountain villages caused the civilian residents, in most part the Christian community, to leave their homes in total panic and disarray. The contexts in which the photographs were taken are not known; each might reflect an individual case at a particular moment in time, or might be staged for the poster. Yet the photographic representations, combined with their textual labelling, ap-pear to be objectively presenting the viewer with facts that reinforce and legitimize the hostile imaginary. *This is who our enemy is*: traditional Druze, savage aggressor, lunatic murderer, and *this is who we are*: pious Christians, righteous, disciplined, modern military forces. The denoted codes brought by the photographs naturalize the connoted message of the poster: *we are inherently different from them*. The constructed connotations are hidden under the appearance of given realities: *our military forces are a legitimate protection from their irrational aggression*.[6]

The Kataeb party's subsumption of violent acts under its discourse of self-protection is subverted in a poster produced by the Lebanese National Movement (fig. 5.3). The image at the centre of the composition features a skull, the ubiquitous symbol of death, stabbed by a blood-dripping dagger, whose handle is replaced by the Kataeb party cedar tree emblem. The poster reveals the names of Palestinian refugee camps and destitute areas in the eastern suburbs of Beirut on whose residents brutal force had been inflicted from 1976 to 1979. The Kataeb party maintained that the violent acts were a legitimate communal response to the threat that these camps posed to the security of the surrounding Christian community in east Beirut. The handwritten town names on the poster are set against a destroyed cityscape covered in a blood-like red haze spreading out from the central skull. The poster title 'Self-security', juxtaposed to an image revealing opposite meanings – aggression, death and mass violence – is intended to overturn the justification claimed by the Kataeb party for exercising military power. Unlike in the previous posters, the enemy here is denied any human traits: it is a faceless criminal, an abstract entity recognized by its political symbol, an agent of death and destruction that resorts to sly political rhetoric to justify its criminal acts.

Representing local foes as agents for foreign enemies of the nation in the context of a civil war is yet another means to intensify the estrangement of the other and widen the internal divide. The local opponent is alienated from the community, portrayed as treacherous and identified through symbols of communal hostility normally attributed to foreign entities. 'On 21 March 1976, the Murabitun destroyed the symbol of fascist treason and took an oath of continuing the journey at whatever cost' (fig. 5.4). The poster commemorates the takeover of the Holiday Inn in Beirut – a hotel that had previously been controlled by the Lebanese Front, mainly by the Kataeb's militia – after fierce and notorious battles in the hotel district, near the waterfront in the city centre. The caricature-style illustration, anchored by the quotation, refers to the destruction of a Western capitalist icon (the Holiday Inn was part of the international hotel chain), 'the symbol of fascist treason', and the poster implies the downfall of the opposing camp.

Another poster condemns the 'Kataeb rule', identified by the two Gemayel brothers' consecutive reign as presidents of Lebanon (fig. 5.5). Bashir Gemayel, asassinated 22 days after his election to the presidency in 1982, was followed by his brother Amin Gemayel. Both were high officials in the Kataeb party and sons of the party founder and leader Pierre Gemayel. The title *Bashir al-damar, Amin al-dollar* ('Preacher of destruction, guardian of the dollar') is both a linguistic twist on their names and a denunciation of their administration supported by an incriminating image. A map of Lebanon has its southern end occupied by a portrait of Bashir Gemayel inscribed within the Star of David (the symbol generally used for Israel), alluding to Bashir's ascendancy to presidency during the 1982 Israeli invasion of Lebanon. The upper part of the map is taken up by a US one-dollar bill in which Amin Gemayel's portrait replaces that of George Washington. The association of Amin with the dollar refers to the depreciation of the Lebanese pound during his presidential rule. The poster vilifies both presidents by constructing relations of equivalence between them and foreign symbols of local communal hatred, one as an agent of Israeli aggression and the other as an economic instrument of 'imperial power' subjugating the population to poverty.

The enemy abstracted into a faceless aggressor devoid of any human traits, a death machine, is a recurrent portrayal of the Israeli army by the local factions involved in resisting Israeli occupation. The blue Star of David, depicted as a menacing force, is a generally used symbol to connote the Israeli enemy. For a Westerner the appropriation of this symbol carries negative connotations and might be seen as a sign of anti-Semitism, because the Star of David was used to identify and persecute Jews during the Second World War. However, in the context of the Arab–Israeli conflict, the Star of David as intended on these posters refers directly to the state of Israel, because it is the central symbol on the Israeli flag. A poster signed by the Islamic Resistance (Hizbullah's military arm) commemorates the massacre of a village in the south of Lebanon. The central figure shows a dead civilian, his body slumping out of a window frame. The illustration implies that all the victims whose portraits and names we see at the bottom of the poster have died in a similar manner: defensively in their homes. An aggressive ring of blood-red rifles with protruding bayonets designates the perpetrator of the massacre; each of the knives closing in on the central victim figure holds the mark of the Star of David. The poster makes a clear division between victims with recognizable faces and names and the enemy as a dehumanized aggressor portrayed through violent weapons (fig. 5.6).

Israel as 'a dehumanized death machine' is conveyed in yet another violent poster. With the title 'The new Nazism passed through South Lebanon', the poster equates Israeli aggression to the Holocaust (fig. 5.7). By way of subversion, the poster names the victims of the Holocaust as the new perpetrators of crimes against humanity. The image reveals the Nazi swastika inside the blue Star of David, tied to six bloody battleaxes. The blood-dripping axes are themselves figures of ancient horror mythologies of death – death has most commonly been popularly personified as a faceless figure dressed in a black robe, head covered and holding a battleaxe to capture life away. The poster image encircled by a black frame thus forms a mechanical wheel of death. Such images of a faceless and powerful aggressor consolidate emotions of fear and resentment of the enemy.

Communal resistance

Against the image of a dehumanized aggressor portrayed through cold machines of war stands the image of a people's resistance. Posters concretize the polarity of 'us' vs 'them' and transform the threatened community into the image of an active defiant one, heroically resisting the enemy. The representation of communal resistance against Israeli assaults on Lebanon has involved concepts of a 'self' that is culturally rooted and that holds natural ties to the land. 'We will resist' titles a poster by the Lebanese National Resistance Front issued in 1983. It represents an imposing figure of a man in heroic confrontation with reticent Israeli rifles (see the small Star of David marked on each) (fig. 5.8). The figure's black moustache and traditional keffiyeh, symbols of ethnic identification and Arab male pride, concretize the 'We' of the poster title, who 'will resist' an enemy *stranger* to the land and culture. The heroic man is drawn with an exaggerated arm held up defiantly to form a clenched fist, the historic icon of left-wing dissent. Here, in a black-and-white drawing set against a raging red, lethal weapons are defied by icons of male strength and popular uprising.

In another poster dating to the early 1980s, a clenched fist shoots up from the ground to defy a shadowed depiction of an Israeli warplane releasing bombs from a reddened sky (fig. 5.9). This poster presents an even more romanticized image of the self. It represents popular resistance, symbolized again by the clenched fist, firmly rooted in the ground like a tree. The enemy, a dark shadow, a modern machine of war, is confronted with the firmness of a people naturally tied to their land. The portrayal of the Israeli army as a war machine through symbols of modern warfare technology – rifles, fighter planes and air raids – recurs in many posters (see figs 5.8–5.12). In most such posters a threatening enemy with sophisticated modern military apparatus is opposed by a civilian communal resistance that fuels its power through icons of collective cultural identification and human strength.

The imaginary of popular resistance is coupled with the notion of civilian resoluteness. It is referred to in Arabic as *sumud*, a charged word that signifies a form of perseverant steadfastness. Through recurrent use in political rhetoric, popular resistance songs and posters, the word has been tied to political connotations of civilian forms of resistance. The concept of *sumud* is also expressed visually in posters. The clenched fist firmly tied to the land, in the above-mentioned poster, is one way of portraying the idea of civilian steadfastness – standing firm in one's land as an act of defiance to the invading enemy. Other posters equally allude to this concept, summoning all members of the community – men, women and children – to be active participants in a communal struggle. A poster by the Organization of Communist Action in the early 1980s warmly portrays a family formed of mother, father and young child holding on to their home, a small house in local vernacular architecture, beneath an Israeli raid. The title cynically affirms 'The American–Israeli "peace" in Lebanon' (fig. 5.12). Another one by the Amal movement, issued around the mid-1980s, features a comic-book-style illustration of a battlefield where members of a community stand up defiantly to an air raid, crushing the very symbol of Israel with their bare hands (fig. 5.10). Such images aspire to empower a community by consolidating the imaginary of unwavering communal solidarity that challenges the advanced military technology of the enemy.

Among Keen's above-mentioned archetypes is the portrayal of the enemy as the enemy of God, which not only legitimizes a hostile imagination of the other but also sanctifies its resistance. Aligned with that is the belief that 'God is on our side' and He will therefore help 'us' in 'our' struggle. A poster by the Amal movement is an example of such belief, concretized through an allegorical image of a religious story supported by the corresponding Koranic verse (fig. 5.11). The verse refers to a divine intervention that saved the Kaaba, the holy Muslim shrine, from an enemy's assault when its custodians could not resist the powerful enemy army. A shower of stones dropped by flocks of birds destroyed the invaders. The narrative of this divine intervention is transposed into the Lebanese context where the illustration depicts a shower of stones destroying the Israeli army. Coupling this with the slogan 'Resistance . . . resistance . . . until liberation', the authors of the poster claim that God is on the side of the resistance.

In all cases, communal resistance is portrayed as a heroic one, symbolically overpowering the foreign enemy. Yet each local camp's articulation of the symbols of communal power is at odds with the others'. Communal resistance in the poster representations of the Lebanese Front, in fact, takes on a different set of iconography. It is tied to a conception of 'we' as defenders of the Lebanese nation and its sovereignty against foreign armed forces present on its territories, particularly the Palestinian organizations and the Syrian army. Unlike posters of resistance against

Israeli occupation, where cultural heritage and ties to the land are emphasized, here symbols of the modern Lebanese nation state are instead brought to the fore: namely the cedar tree (in reference to the Lebanese flag) and the map of Lebanon, pertaining to national sovereignty. These signs are aligned with the previously discussed LF self-image as a modern community opposed to an enemy imagined as backward and tribal.

Coming back to a poster discussed earlier in which the ADF (including its Syrian army majority) are designated as 'the Arab barbaric tribes', the poster's message is centred on the resistance and steadfastness of Ain el-Rummaneh, affirmed in the main title 'The world is asleep while Ain el-Rummaneh stays awake' (fig. 5.13). Ain el-Rummaneh, an area in the eastern Christian sector of Beirut's periphery situated on the green line that divided the capital into two sectors, holds a great deal of value for the Lebanese Front in particular and for the Christian sectarian consciousness in general. It was the site where the civil war officially began in 1975. It was also an area that witnessed intense bombardment in 1978 by the Syrian army. The town is personified as a modern residential building wearing combat gear, heavily wounded yet gigantic, crushing a belittled opponent labelled as 'the Arab barbaric tribes'. Communal resistance in this poster is a combination between a civil resistance (the residential building personifying Ain el-Rummaneh) and a military one (the building wearing combat boots). Such combined forms of communal resistance recur in LF posters conveying a self-image of a civilian populace militarized against its enemies. The poster's overall cartoon-style narrative is a literal visualization of a popular expression: 'We [LF] carry on our back the Lebanese cause, and hold the flame of belief in Lebanon'. The same expression is visualized in yet another poster, with the title 'Towards independence' (fig. 5.16). The illustration is peculiar in its style of rendering, being made up of coloured square modules. Produced in 1980, it could be an allusion to the low-resolution video games of the time or simply based on a squared notebook; in either case the image conveys a modern aesthetic.

Displacement and belonging

Imagining a community is also about that which is remembered, narratives that attach communities to places of belonging they call 'home'. Particularly when their experience of 'home' has been severed, these places become themselves subject to appropriation of a collective imaginary ripe with images and symbols. It is 'not only about what is remembered but how and in what form', Edward Said notes in his essay 'Invention, memory, and place'. 'It is an issue about the very fraught nature of representation, not just about content.'[7] Representations of places of belonging are not passive perceptions of an individual's remembrance, they are images endowed with political meaning ascribing to a collective memory in which past events have been selected, reconstructed and maintained as sites of collective identification.[8] In this way, collective memory of a place of belonging secures a coherent identity and narrative of a displaced community, builds hope and mobilizes its people around a shared motive, to return 'home'.

Displacement was common practice among the different communities in war-time Lebanon. Families left their homes temporarily to seek safer havens in and out-side Lebanon depending on their economic conditions. Although these movements were destabilizing for most who endured them, they do not represent a traumatic loss of 'home' like the cases of forced displacement resulting from violent expulsion and military occupation. In such cases the notion of 'lost territory', specific to battle-fields, overlaps that of 'lost home' and impregnates it with political meaning. For the desire to return 'home' necessitates a struggle to reclaim a lost territory.

Displacement and belonging characterized the discourse of various Lebanese political factions at decisive moments in the unfolding events of the war. Posters did their part in instituting and diffusing representations of places of belonging. As I argued earlier in this chapter, the demarcation of a hostile enemy is necessary for the construction of a collective identity. I would add to the argument that images of places of belonging equally serve as politically loaded sites in a given hegemonic struggle. They secure collective identification with a place/home and mobilize a community to reclaim a lost home/territory. Iconography of heritage, folklore, village tradition, nature and landscape consolidates a collective imaginary of a past 'home' imbued with a history of communal practices connected to it. The posters of communal resistance to Israel discussed earlier are replete with signs of cultural belonging coupled with the concept of steadfastness and attachment to land. The image of the enemy is not always present in posters representing places of belonging, yet it is not entirely absent. It is inevitably implied as being the cause of the community's displacement and suffering.

The south

'The south' is a loaded linguistic sign, referring to several layers of cultural, economic and political signifieds, all condensed in this one word. In terms of Lebanon's natural geography, the south is known as a fertile landscape of agricultural fields, which has created specific economic and social practices related to land cultivation. On the level of political economy, as a rural area it has historically suffered from deprivation and neglect by the state in terms of development plans. Politically, with the rise of the

Palestinian resistance movements in the late 1960s the south became a stronghold of guerrilla operations on the border with Israel. It has since then acquired a symbolic political status tied to a liberation struggle within the Arab–Israeli conflict. The first Israeli invasion of South Lebanon in 1978, continued air raids, and subsequent occupation in 1982 reaffirmed 'the south' as *the icon* of national resistance in the discourse of Arab struggle with Israel. A poster published by the Lebanese National Movement around 1980 symbolically highlights the occupied territory of South Lebanon on a map of the Arab world (fig. 5.17). The image illustrates the poster title that metaphorically affirms: 'The Arab sun rises from the south'. The layers of meaning constructed around the idea of 'the south' render it a loaded symbol, where the politics of resistance and class struggle overlap with images of fertile landscape. Symbolic representations of 'the south' endow scenery of landscape and nature with politically and emotionally charged signs of belonging, thereby actively summoning resistance and liberation struggle. 'The south' has thus been the subject of many posters by different political factions, prominent artists as well as civil resistance organizations (see chapter 1).

The collective imaginary constructed around 'the south' is intensely represented in a number of posters featuring people as integral to the land and nature. Their bodies form a natural continuation of the landscape, often in overwhelming symbolic imagery. Two examples of posters will illustrate this concept of 'natural' belonging, whereby two entities (land and people) are intrinsic to one another and therefore hard to dissociate. Both posters were issued following the first Israeli invasion in 1978. The first, by the Nasserist organization al-Murabitun, shows a hand deeply ingrained in the soil of a green mountainous landscape in whose depths lie little villages (fig. 5.18). The scale of the hand is exaggerated to seem closer to that of the mountain, forming a continuation of its lines and curves, while little drops of blood are scattered around the fingers and arm. Anchored by the title 'Steadfast in the south', the poster visualizes the firm, enduring resistance to separation from a natural habitat. The second poster, by the Lebanese National Movement, portrays a crowd of what seem like armed civilians standing proudly with their Kalashnikovs held up (fig. 5.19). Beneath the fighters lies the poster title 'The south', its letters drawn to seem as if carved out of solid rock. A yellow cast fills both rock and crowd against the striking red of the poster's background. The yellow unites the two entities into a whole – 'the south' and its people, the solid rock and its custodians.

'Our mountain'

In an altogether different geographic location and political circumstances, the massive displacement of the Christian community from their mountain villages formed the subject matter of a series of posters mostly produced by the Lebanese Forces, presenting again a quite distinct type of iconography of resistance and 'home'.

The displacement, occurring mainly between 1983 and 1984, was a consequence of fierce battles that took hold in the mountains between the Christian and Druze communities, led respectively by the Lebanese Forces and the Progressive Socialist Party militias. The mountain battles resulted in major losses for the LF, which caused their withdrawal from what became PSP-controlled territories. At the time, media efforts increased and more posters were issued to mobilize the LF combatants. These posters reaffirmed the need for the Christian community's militarized resistance, actively defending its threatened 'home' and existence in the region. Mount Lebanon has been the Christian community and its dominant Maronite majority's historical home and refuge across centuries in the Middle East region.

The period of the mountain battles coincided with a communal state of apathy that followed the assassination, in 1982, of Bashir Gemayel, who was military commander of the Lebanese Forces and short-lived president of Lebanon (see chapter 2). The persistent slogan *Bashir hayy fina liyabqa Lubnan* ('Bashir lives in us so that Lebanon remains') was drawn into an emblem, used in a campaign of posters addressed to the LF combatants and the threatened Christian community at large. One of these posters depicts a stencilled icon of a geared-up fighter ready for combat (fig. 5.20). The combatant icon is repeated around the LF logo, which forms the central subject of the poster composition. In the lower part of the poster lies a landscape of mountains with a rising sun. The composition uses the same elements as the 'Bashir lives in us' emblem, present in the bottom-left corner. The three lines of the poster slogan 'Comrade . . . you are heroism, you are faith, with you Lebanon remains' are excerpts from a mainly textual poster (fig. 5.21), part of the same campaign, hailing the noble combatant as the custodian of a threatened Christian community:

> My resisting comrade:
> . . . With your steadfastness, you preserved our free Christian existence in this region.
> You are the shield of our Christian people and the guarantee for its continued existence, if you fall, it falls.
> Our continued existence is therefore subject to your faith and steadfastness. . . .
> Bashir lives in us so that *our Lebanon* remains [my emphasis]

The icon of the all-geared-up combatant comes again in another poster (fig. 5.22). It is depicted in a more detailed illustration closely resembling the previous one in silhouette and posture, but instead of dynamically approaching, as if ready for combat, it seems firmly grounded in place. The statement 'Here we remain' anchors the firmness in the image. 'Here' is indicated in the landscape behind the combatant figure: mountains housing a picturesque Lebanese village with traditional red-tiled-roof stone houses, green trees and a village church. The ensemble of selected symbols of heritage, faith and landscape constructs the iconography of a romanticized 'village home'. It thus materializes an image of collective imaginary of a place of belonging for the displaced Christian community.

A logo-icon representing the village was designed holding these same symbols with the addition of a farmer ploughing the land and a village well, *'ayn*, symbols typically present in popular folk tales, poetry and songs alluding to a Mount Lebanon heritage. The icon, accompanied by the inscription 'Our mountain: man, land and heritage', was circulated in LF magazines as well as in their posters, consolidating the representation and claim over home/territory (fig. 5.23). 'The Christmas of "our mountain" children' is the title of a poster featuring the icon as its central image. Children with patched-up clothes, alluding to the state of poverty caused by displacement, walk on a path that leads them to 'our mountain', affirmed by the statement 'Next holiday will be in the village'. The poster is hopeful in its message yet its affirmation underlines the struggle needed to accomplish the children's resolutely symbolic aspiration to celebrate Christmas 'at home' (fig. 5.24).

Concluding remarks

The various posters discussed above reveal the articulations of a political community's struggle, where imaginaries of communal self in relation to a hostile enemy are symbolically concretized through images. However, as exemplified in these cases, the constructions of communal belonging have varied with the types of political struggle. On a final note, at the risk of sounding reductive of the complex interpretations outlined above, some comparative concluding remarks can be drawn.

The claim over 'the south' and the struggle with Israel has mostly been represented as a popular resistance against a highly militarized enemy. The self is symbolically articulated through an intrinsic relation between a people and their land, where politically charged signs of landscape and cultural heritage are emphasized. This cultural affirmation of the self is opposed to an abstracted representation of Israel as a dehumanized modern machine of war, a fearful image of an enemy without a face. While maintaining cultural locality, the image of the south is not drawn in narrow geographic terms limited to Lebanese territories. The resistance to occupation of South Lebanon is linked to regional struggle and national imaginaries in which Israel is demarcated as the hostile other. This is indicated in the above-mentioned poster by the LNM that highlights South Lebanon in the map of the Arab world. As discussed in previous chapters, the SSNP ideologically ties its resistance in Lebanon to a greater struggle of reclaiming 'natural Syria'; equally, Hizbullah's resistance is inscribed in the liberation of the Muslim *Umma* (see figs 3.1, 3.3 and 3.28).

At the same time, the internal struggle over the mountain home/territory is strongly militarized. The Lebanese Forces posters advance a typology of a disciplined warrior mobilized to protect a Christian community's existence. This self-image is set against that of an enemy portrayed as a backward savage aggressor, as seen in the poster featuring the Druze 'murderer' vs the Christian 'combatant' (see fig. 5.2). The posters designed during the mountain battles share with the earlier ones – issued by the Lebanese Front around 1978 incriminating the ADF and Syria in particular – a similar typology of derogatory representations of the enemy that are opposed to an advanced self (barbaric/tribal vs modern/national and savage/aggressor vs civilized/military). Despite the continuous claim of civilized superiority over their adversaries, a transformation can be noted in the self-image of the Lebanese Front. The change can be traced in relation to the shifting struggle and type of enemy against which the self is demarcated. The iconography of the late 1970s posters relied on national symbols (the flag and map of Lebanon) advancing the image of a modern Lebanese state. The imaginary frontiers of the community's political identity in relation to the enemy were drawn at the level of national borders, a map of Lebanon secluded from its environment. Conversely, in the internal struggle over the mountains from 1983 to 1984, symbols of heritage, village tradition and religion prevail to form essential components of the same political community's identity and belonging.

This is not only indicative of how identities are constituted through political struggle but also seems to bring about a paradox. We might argue that these are conflicting self-representations. One is modern and national, it affirms 'I am Lebanese,' and the other is traditional and parochial, 'I am Christian from the mountain villages.' However, these self-representations are tightly linked. In the conception of the former, the continuity of the modern project of the Lebanese nation state was claimed to be at stake; while the assertion of the latter embodies fear of a disruption in the very narrative that led to the formation of the Lebanese nation. The modern Lebanese state (post-1920 Greater Lebanon) was in fact created as an extension of the Mount Lebanon district, where a sense of Lebanese identity and homeland emerged among the ruling Maronites. This is to say that within the dominant discourse of the Christian Maronite community, the loss of the mountain village 'home' disrupts the claim over the national one. 'Our mountain' is after all integral to 'our Lebanon'.

A similar transformation in the representation of the self can be seen in the Progressive Socialist Party around the same time during the mountain battles. The

PSP's victory in the mountains was commemorated in 1984 through a quite blatant poster, which was issued in the context of the annual commemoration of the assassination of Kamal Jumblatt, the party founder, on 16 March (fig. 5.25). It features a large photograph of a young teenage boy, walking confidently with a Kalashnikov in his hands, a smile of content lighting up his face. The brief yet evocative title directs the meaning of the image and frames the overall poster message within the discourse of a community's self-protection: *Ibn al-jabal* ('The mountain's upbringing'). The poster proclaims, in tribute to its lost leader, the community's pride in the nurturing of fearless young boys who will rise to its protection and support. Furthermore, Kamal Jumblatt 'the symbol of progressive and secular Arab Lebanon' transformed into a parochial Druze *za'im* in the poster featuring his portrait accompanied by symbols of the Druze sect and mountain traditions (fig. 2.14).

The struggle over 'our mountain', in both the Lebanese Forces and the Progressive Socialist Party discourses, was structured on the basis of confessional identities. The articulation of these identities brought to the fore memories of ancient violent feuds between the Druze and Christians in Mount Lebanon dating to the mid-nineteenth century. The constructed frontiers in each of the communities' imaginary in relation to one another seemed ancient, uninterrupted and intrinsic to 'their mountain' belonging.

NOTES

Foreword: Posters as Weapons

1   Bredekamp, Horst, 'Bildakte als Zeugnis und Urteil', in Monika Flacke (ed.), *Mythen der Nationen. 1945 – Arena der Erinnerungen*, Vol. I (Mainz, 2004).

Introduction: Political Posters as Symbolic Sites of Struggle

1   Crowley, David, 'The propaganda poster', in Margaret Timmers (ed.), *The Power of the Poster* (London: V&A Publications, 1998), pp. 100–1.

2   Crowley: 'The propaganda poster', pp. 115–16.

3   Crowley: 'The propaganda poster', p. 129.

4   Chomsky, Noam, *Media Control: The Spectacular Achievements of Propaganda*, 2nd edn. (New York: Seven Stories Press, 2002), p. 37.

5   Crowley: 'The propaganda poster', pp. 134–6.

6   McQuiston, Liz, *Graphic Agitation: Social and Political Graphics Since the Sixties* (London: Phaidon, 2004), p. 28.

7   Chomsky, Noam and Edward S. Herman, *Manufacturing Consent: The Political Economy of the Mass Media* (New York: Vintage, 1998), pp. 1–2.

8   Jowett, Garth and Victoria O'Donnell, *Propaganda and Persuasion*, 3rd edn. (London: Sage Publications, 1999), p. 6.

9   Garth and O'Donnell: *Propaganda and Persuasion*, p. 11.

10   Garth and O'Donnell: *Propaganda and Persuasion*, p. 23.

11   Garth and O'Donnell: *Propaganda and Persuasion*, p. 7.

12   Garth and O'Donnell: *Propaganda and Persuasion*, p. 9.

13   Douglas Kellner writes: 'the focus of British cultural studies at any given moment was mediated by the struggles in the present political conjuncture and their major work was thus conceived as political interventions. Their studies of ideology, domination and resistance, and the politics of culture, directed cultural studies toward analyzing cultural artifacts, practices, and institutions within existing networks of power and of showing how culture both provided tools and forces of domination and resources for resistance and struggle.' Kellner, Douglas, *Media Culture: Cultural Studies, Identity and Politics Between the Modern and the Postmodern* (London: Routledge, 1995), p. 36.

14   Hall, Stuart, 'Encoding/decoding', in Stuart Hall, Dorothy Hobson, Andrew Lowe and Paul Willis (eds), *Culture, Media, Language* (London: Routledge, 1980), p. 131.

15   Hall: 'Encoding/decoding', p. 132.

16   Barthes, Roland, *Image Music Text*, trans. Stephen Heath (London: Fontana Press, 1977), p. 36.

17   See Barthes, Roland, *Mythologies* (New York: Hill and Wang, 1983).

18   Barthes: *Image Music Text*, p. 45.

19   Barthes: *Image Music Text*, p. 51.

20   Hall: 'Encoding/decoding', p. 131.

21   Hall: 'Encoding/decoding', p. 129.

22   Grossberg, Lawrence, 'On post-modernism and articulation: an interview with Stuart Hall', in David Morley and Kuan-Hsing Chen (eds), *Stuart Hall: Critical Dialogues in Cultural Studies* (London: Routledge, 1996), p. 141.

23   Hall's use of articulation builds on the development of a theory of articulation by Ernesto Laclau in his book *Politics and Ideology in Marxist Theory*. See Grossberg: 'On post-modernism and articulation', p. 142.

24   Laclau, Ernesto and Chantal Mouffe, *Hegemony and Socialist Strategy: Towards a Radical Democratic Politics*, 2nd edn. (London: Verso, 2001), p. 105. Their concept of 'articulation' builds on Louis Althusser's logic of overdetermination. Laclau and Mouffe observe overdetermination as 'the field of contingent variation as opposed to an essential determination . . . the field of identities, which never manage to be fully fixed', pp. 99–111.

25   Laclau and Mouffe: *Hegemony and Socialist Strategy*, pp. 105–6.

26   Hall: 'Encoding/decoding', p. 134.

27   Hall: 'Encoding/decoding', pp. 135–6.

28   Hall: 'Encoding/decoding', pp. 136–8.

29   Laclau and Mouffe: *Hegemony and Socialist Strategy*, pp. 66–7.

30   Williams, Raymond, *Marxism and Literature* (Oxford: Oxford University Press, 1977), p. 112.

31   Foucault, Michel, 'Truth and power', in *Power/Knowledge: Selected Interviews and Other Writings, 1972–1977* (New York: Pantheon Books, 1980), p. 131.

32   Foucault: 'Truth and power', p. 131.

33   Douglas Kellner for instance notes: 'The concept of hegemony, rather than that of propaganda, better characterizes the specific nature of commercial television in the United States. Whereas propaganda has the connotation of self-conscious, heavy-handed, intentional, and coercive manipulation, hegemony has the connotation more appropriate to television, of induced consent, of a more subtle process of in-corporating individuals into patterns of belief and behavior.' In Kellner, Douglas, *Television and the Crisis of Democracy* (Boulder, CO: Westview, 1990), pp. 19–20, as quoted in Stanley Cunningham, *The Idea of Propaganda: A Reconstruction* (Westport, CT: Praeger Publishers, 2002).

34   Laclau and Mouffe: *Hegemony and Socialist Strategy*, pp. 139–43.

35   Laclau and Mouffe claim that 'articulatory practices take place not only within given social political spaces, but between them'; Laclau and Mouffe: *Hegemony and Socialist Strategy*, p. 140.

Chapter 1: Agents, Aesthetic Genres and Localities

1   Some parties ran their own radio broadcast station and a few established a television station in the 1980s. These broadcast media had their own institutional setting sep-arate from the party's media office.

2   The account is based on interviews held with party media officials and poster design-ers between 2005 and 2006.

3   The calligraphic banner, *yafta*, is a hand-painted message on a large cloth 5 to 8 metres wide, which would be either fixed within a street or carried by hand by wooden sticks on both ends during a public march.

4   Traboulsi, Fawwaz, *A History of Modern Lebanon* (London: Pluto Press, 2007), p. 169.

5   See Rabi'i, Shawkat al-, *al-Fan al-Tashkili fi al-Fikr al-Arabi al-Thawri (Art in Arab Revolutionary Thought)* (Iraq: Ministry of Culture and Information, Dar el-Rashid, Art Series, 1979); Azzawi, Dia' al-, *The Art of Posters in Iraq, a study of its beginning and development 1938–1973* (Iraq: Ministry of Culture and Information, Dar el-Rashid, Art Series, 1974); Bahnisi, Afif, *Al-Fan wal-Qawmiya (Art and Nationalism)* (Damascus: Ministry of Culture and National Guidance, 1965).

6   *Al-Fan al-Iraqi al-Mu'asser (Contemporary Iraqi Art)*, volume 1 – visual arts (Lausanne: Sartek, 1977).

7   Ali, Wijdan, 'Modern Arab art: an overview', in Salwa Mikdadi Nashashibi (ed.), *Forces of Change: Artists of the Arab World* (Lafayette, CA: International Council for Women in the Arts, 1994), pp. 73–4.

8   Kameel Hawa established al-Mohtaraf, an acclaimed graphic design firm, based in Saudi Arabia and Lebanon.

9   For more information on OSPAAAL and other protest posters see Cushing, Lincoln, ¡Revolución! Cuban Poster Art (San Francisco: Chronicle Books, 2003); Frick, Richard (ed.), The Tricontinental Solidarity Poster (Bern: Comedia-Verlag, 2003); and Martin, Susan (ed.), Decade of Protest: Political Posters from the United States, Vietnam, Cuba 1965–1975 (California: Smart Art Press, 1996).

10   Frick (ed.): The Tricontinental Solidarity Poster, p. 92.

11   In an interview with the author, July 2006.

12   In an interview with the author, January 2006.

13   In an interview with the author, February 2007.

14   Moussalli remained active until very recently, when his old age and eye problems did not permit him to pursue his painting with the same ardency and as new means of design and digital printing took over the market of leaders' portraits.

15   Muhammad Ismail established after 1994 his own independent graphic design studio and continued to provide his services to Hizbullah's media office on a consultancy basis.

16   See Chelkowski, Peter and Hamid Dabashi, Staging a Revolution: The Art of Persuasion in the Islamic Republic of Iran (London: Booth-Clibborn Editions, 1999).

17   For further study on Hizbullah's allegiance to Wilayat al-Faqih, see Saad-Ghorayeb, Amal, Hizbu'llah: Politics and Religion (London: Pluto Press, 2002), pp. 64–8.

18   Chelkowski and Dabashi: Staging a Revolution, p. 115.

Chapter 2: Leadership

1   Heller, Steven, 'Designing heroes', Eye 43 (Spring 2002), p. 49.

2   Falasca-Zamponi, Simonetta, Fascist Spectacle: The Aesthetics of Power in Mussolini's Italy (Berkeley: University of California Press, 2000), p. 86.

3   Poynor, Rick, 'A symbol returns to its true colours', Eye 40 (Summer 2001), p. 8.

4   Heller: 'Designing heroes', p. 49.

5   Hanf, Theodore, Coexistence in Wartime Lebanon: Decline of a State and Rise of a Nation (London: Centre for Lebanese Studies in association with I.B.Tauris, 1993), p. 181.

6   See Hottinger, Arnold, 'Zu'ama' in historical perspective', in Leonard Binder (ed.), Politics in Lebanon (New York: Wiley, 1996); Gilsenan, Michael, 'Against patron–client relations', Khalaf, Samir, 'Changing forms of political patronage in Lebanon', and Johnson, Michael, 'Political bosses and their gangs: zu'ama and qabadayat in the Sunni Muslim quarters of Beirut', in Ernest Gellner and John Waterbury (eds), Patrons and Clients in Mediterranean Societies (London: Duckworth, 1977).

7   Hottinger: 'Zu'ama' in historical perspective', p. 85.

8   Khalaf, Samir, *Lebanon's Predicament* (New York: Columbia University Press, 1987), p. 98.

9   Such forms of political patronage are still practised today to a large extent.

10   Khazen, Farid el-, *The Breakdown of the State in Lebanon, 1967–1976* (London: I.B.Tauris, 2000), p. 52.

11   See *Kamal Jumblatt 1917–1977, Al-Rajul wal-Massira*, published by the media committee for the commemoration of Jumblatt's international day: 1 May 1977.

12   Khazen, Farid el-, 'Kamal Jumblatt, the uncrowned Druze prince of the left', *Middle Eastern Studies* xxiv/2 (April 1988), p. 199.

13   Abou, Selim, *Bechir Gemayel, ou, L'esprit d'un peuple* (Paris: Editions Anthropos, 1984), p. 14.

14   Abou: *Bechir Gemayel*, p. 27.

15   Khalaf: *Lebanon's Predicament*, p. 89.

16   The poster created by the American illustrator James Montgomery Flagg in 1917 is in fact based on an older British version designed by Alfred Leete in 1914. The design became a prototype used in many countries for recruitment purposes, including the USSR, Germany and Italy; see Heller: 'Designing heroes'. It had also been locally adapted by the PLO faction PFLP in a campaign denouncing the Egyptian president Anwar el-Sadat's signing of the Camp David peace accord with Israel.

17   'C'est de la présence de l'Absent dans la mémoire et le Coeur de chacun que l'on devait tirer le courage de poursuivre l'oeuvre commencée'. Abou: *Bechir Gemayel*, p. 31.

18   An example of this in the printed media is *al-Massira (The Procession)*, an LF periodical, started in 1982. Aimed mainly at an audience of combatants in the first two years of its publication, in 1985 it developed into a large-audience magazine. In its first two years it featured in each issue a small poster-like portrait of Bashir Gemayel and recalled his statements in colloquial Arabic.

19   Abou: *Bechir Gemayel*, p. 45.

20   In *Mithaq Harakat al Mahroumin* (the charter of the Movement of the Disinherited), as quoted in Halawi, Majed, *Against the Current: The Political Mobilization of the Shi'a Community in Lebanon* (Ann Arbor, MI: UMI Dissertation Information Service, 1996), p. 246.

21   Halawi: *Against the Current*, pp. 206–8.

22   Tueni, Ghassan, *Une guerre pour les autres* (Paris: Jean-Claude Lattès, 1985), pp. 97–8, as quoted in Fouad Ajami, *The Vanished Imam* (Ithaca, NY: Cornell University Press, 1986), p. 49.

23   See Halawi: *Against the Current*.

24   As quoted in Halawi: *Against the Current*, p. 245.

25   The documentary *Ahzab Lubnan (Parties of Lebanon)* (Beirut: NBN, 2002).

26   The quote is from Mussa al-Sadr's acclaimed public speech in Baalbek officially pro-
      claiming Amal as the military wing of the Movement of the Disinherited.

Chapter 3: Commemoration

1   Said, Edward, 'Invention, memory, and place', in W.J.T. Mitchell (ed.), *Landscape and
      Power* (Chicago: University of Chicago Press, 2002), p. 251.
2   See Pipes, Daniel, 'Radical politics and the Syrian Social Nationalist Party', *International
      Journal of Middle East Studies* xx/3 (August 1988).
3   Saadeh, Antun, *al-Muhadarat al'Asher 1948 (The Ten Lectures 1948)* (Beirut: Syrian Social
      Nationalist Party, n.d.).
4   See Stoakes, Frank, 'The supervigilantes: the Lebanese Kataeb Party as a builder, sur-
      rogate and defender of the state', *Middle Eastern Studies* xi/3 (October 1975).
5   The Mount Lebanon *Mutasarrifiya* is a self-ruled administrative council, established
      by the Ottomans in 1860, in which governance and political power was attributed to
      the Maronites. For detailed accounts of the Maronites' relation to the Lebanese state,
      see Khazen, Farid el-, *The Breakdown of the State in Lebanon, 1967–1976* (London: I.B.Tauris,
      2000), pp. 33–40; and Aulas, Marie-Christine, 'The socio-ideological development of
      the Maronite community: the emergence of the Phalanges and the Lebanese Forces',
      Arab Studies Quarterly vii/4 (Fall 1985).
6   Salibi, Kamal, 'The Lebanese identity', *Journal of Contemporary History* vi, 'Nationalism
      and Separatism' (1971), p. 78.
7   See Falasca-Zamponi, Simonetta, *Fascist Spectacle: The Aesthetics of Power in Mussolini's Italy*
      (Berkeley: University of California Press, 2000); and Bonnell, Victoria E., *Iconography
      of Power: Soviet Political Posters under Lenin and Stalin* (Berkeley: University of California
      Press, 1997).
8   Anderson, Benedict, *Imagined Communities: Reflections on the Origin and Spread of Nationalism*
      (London: Verso, 1991), pp. 204, 206.
9   In Arabic the two words for 'grave' and 'dawn' rhyme.
10   Hanf, Theodore, *Coexistence in Wartime Lebanon: Decline of a State and Rise of a Nation* (London:
      Centre for Lebanese Studies in association with I.B.Tauris, 1993), p. 251.
11   Hanf: *Coexistence in Wartime Lebanon*, p. 289.
12   *L'affiche Palestinienne: Collection Ezzedine Kalak* (Paris: Le Sycamore, 1979), pp. 38–9.
13   See Grabar, Oleg, *The Dome of the Rock* (Cambridge, MA: Harvard University Press,
      2006).
14   Chelkowski, Peter and Hamid Dabashi, *Staging a Revolution: The Art of Persuasion in the
      Islamic Republic of Iran* (London: Booth-Clibborn Editions, 1999), p. 217.

Chapter 4: Martyrdom

1   Anderson, Benedict, *Imagined Communities: Reflections on the Origin and Spread of Nationalism* (London: Verso, 1991), p. 144.

2   See Ranstorp, Magnus, *Hizb'allah in Lebanon: The Politics of the Western Hostage Crisis* (Hampshire: Macmillan, 1997), p. 38.

3   Quoted in Davis, Joyce M., *Martyrs: Innocence, Vengeance and Despair in the Middle East* (Hampshire: Palgrave Macmillan, 2003), pp. 70–1.

4   In an interview with the author.

5   VHS-format copies of SSNP martyrs' video statements were widely accessible in west Beirut in the mid-eighties, most often in very bad condition, as a result of multiple copying.

6   Saad-Ghorayeb, Amal, *Hizbu'llah: Politics and Religion* (London: Pluto Press, 2002), pp. 121–2.

7   Qassem, Naim, *Hizbollah: The Story from Within*, trans. Dalia Khalil (London: Saqi, 2005), p. 39.

8   Qassem: *Hizbollah*, p. 42.

9   See Saad-Ghorayeb: *Hizbu'llah*.

10 The Dome of the Rock icon is very often mistakenly referred to as Al-Aqsa Mosque: the latter is a different building situated on the same holy site.

11 Jerusalem is known to have been the first kiblah, before Mecca was designated for that purpose.

12 According to Shi'ite narratives, Imam Hussein, son of Imam Ali and grandson of the prophet, while contesting the oppressive and corrupt Umayyad reign was slain in Karbala, along with seventy of his followers, by the Umayyad ruler Yazid Ibn Mu'awiya, in 680 or the year 61 in the Islamic *Hijri* calendar. The Karbala event has marked and formed Shi'ite revolutionary discourse. For detailed studies see Halawi, Majed, *Against the Current: The Political Mobilization of the Shi'a Community in Lebanon* (Ann Arbor, MI: UMI Dissertation Information Service, 1996); and Shams al-Din, Muhammad Mahdi, *Thawrat al Hussein: Zurufuha al-Ijtima'iya wa Atharaha al-Insaniya* (*The Revolution of al-Hussein: Its Social Circumstances and Human Effects*) (Beirut: Dar al-Ta'aruf lil-matbu'at, n.d.).

13 Chelkowski, Peter and Hamid Dabashi, *Staging a Revolution: The Art of Persuasion in the Islamic Republic of Iran* (London: Booth-Clibborn Editions, 1999), p. 74.

14 Halawi: *Against the Current*, p. 262.

15 Qassem: *Hizbollah*, p. 45.

16 See Chelkowski and Dabashi: *Staging a Revolution*.

17 In Khomeini, *Sahifah-Ye Nur* xvi (1982), p. 219, as quoted in Chelkowski and Dabashi: *Staging a Revolution*, p. 277.

18   Saad-Ghorayeb: *Hizbu'llah*, p. 119.

19   See Chelkowski and Dabashi: *Staging a Revolution*, p. 289.

Chapter 5: Belonging

1   Mouffe, Chantal, *On the Political* (London: Routledge, 2005), p. 14.

2   Mouffe: *On the Political*, pp. 15–16.

3   Heller, Steven, 'Designing demons: the rhetoric of hate provides a different kind of meaning', *Eye* 41 (Autumn 2001), p. 44.

4   Keen, Sam, *Faces of the Enemy: Reflections of the Hostile Imagination*, 2nd edn. (San Francisco: Harper and Row, 1988), p. 10.

5   Keen: *Faces of the Enemy*, p. 25.

6   Roland Barthes notes that 'The more technology develops the diffusion of information (and notably of images) the more it provides the means of masking the constructed meaning under the appearance of the given meaning', in *Image Music Text*, trans. Stephen Heath (London: Fontana Press, 1977), p. 47.

7   Said delivered the essay 'Invention, memory, and place' in his keynote address at a conference on 'Landscape perspectives in Palestine' held in 1998 at Bir Zeit University, in the West Bank; in W.J.T. Mitchell (ed.), *Landscape and Power* (Chicago: University of Chicago Press, 2002), p. 242.

8   Said: 'Invention, memory, and place'.

BIBLIOGRAPHY

Theory and method

Anderson, Benedict, *Imagined Communities: Reflections on the Origin and Spread of Nationalism* (London: Verso, 1991)

Barthes, Roland, *Image Music Text*, trans. Stephen Heath (London: Fontana Press, 1977)

Barthes, Roland, *Mythologies* (New York: Hill and Wang, 1983)

Chomsky, Noam, *Media Control: The Spectacular Achievements of Propaganda*, 2nd edn. (New York: Seven Stories Press, 2002)

Chomsky, Noam and Edward S. Herman, *Manufacturing Consent: The Political Economy of the Mass Media* (New York: Vintage, 1998)

Cunningham, Stanley B., *The Idea of Propaganda: A Reconstruction* (Westport, CT: Praeger Publishers, 2002)

Ellul, Jacques, *Propaganda: The Formation of Men's Attitudes* (New York: Alfred A. Knopf, 1968)

Foucault, Michel, *The Archaeology of Knowledge* (New York: Pantheon Books, 1980)

Foucault, Michel, *Power/Knowledge: Selected Interviews and Other Writings, 1972–1977* (New York: Pantheon Books, 1980)

Hall, Stuart (ed.), *Representation: Cultural Representations and Signifying Practices* (London: Sage Publications in association with Open University, 1997)

Hall, Stuart, Dorothy Hobson, Andrew Lowe and Paul Willis (eds), *Culture, Media, Language* (London: Routledge, 1980)

Hobsbawm, Eric and Terence Ranger (eds), *The Invention of Tradition* (Cambridge: Cambridge University Press, 1983)

Jenks, Chris, *Culture*, 2nd edn. (London: Routledge, 2005)

Jowett, Garth and Victoria O'Donnell, *Propaganda and Persuasion*, 3rd edn. (London: Sage Publications, 1999)

Kantorowicz, Ernst H., *The King's Two Bodies: A Study in Mediaeval Political Theology* (Princeton, NJ: Princeton University Press, 1957)

Kellner, Douglas, *Media Culture: Cultural Studies, Identity and Politics Between the Modern and the Postmodern* (London: Routledge, 1995)

Laclau, Ernesto, *New Reflections on the Revolution of Our Time* (London: Verso, 1990)

Laclau, Ernesto and Chantal Mouffe, *Hegemony and Socialist Strategy: Towards a Radical Democratic Politics*, 2nd edn. (London: Verso, 2001)

Laclau, Ernesto (ed.), *The Making of Political Identities* (London: Verso, 1994)

McQuail, Denis, *McQuail's Mass Communication Theory*, 3rd edn. (London: Sage Publications, 2005)

Marris, Paul and Sue Thornham, *Media Studies: A Reader*, 2nd edn. (Edinburgh: Edinburgh University Press, 1999)

Mitchell, W.J.T. (ed.), *Landscape and Power* (Chicago: University of Chicago Press, 2002)

Morley, David and Kuan-Hsing Chen (eds), *Stuart Hall: Critical Dialogues in Cultural Studies* (London: Routledge, 1996)

Mouffe, Chantal, *On the Political* (London: Routledge, 2005)

Procter, James, *Stuart Hall* (London: Routledge, 2004)

Rabinow, Paul (ed.), *The Foucault Reader* (New York: Pantheon Books, 1972)

Rose, Gillian, *Visual Methodologies* (London: Sage Publications, 2001)

Torfing, Jacob, *New Theories of Discourse* (Oxford: Blackwell, 1999)

Williams, Raymond, *Marxism and Literature* (Oxford: Oxford University Press, 1977)

Williams, Raymond, *Keywords: A Vocabulary of Culture and Society* (Oxford: Oxford University Press, 1985)

Williamson, Judith, *Decoding Advertisements: Ideology and Meaning in Advertising* (New York: Marion Boyars, 1978)

Posters and political iconography

Ades, Dawn, *The 20th-Century Poster: Design of the Avant-Garde* (New York: Abbeville Press, 1984)

A'li, Abdulfazl (ed.), *The Graphic Art of the Islamic Revolution* (Tehran: Art Bureau of the Islamic Media Organization, 1985)

Balaghi, Shiva and Lynn Gumpert (eds), *Picturing Iran: Art, Society and Revolution* (London: I.B.Tauris, 2002)

Bartelt, Dana, *Both Sides of Peace: Israeli and Palestinian Political Poster Art* (Raleigh, NC: Contemporary Art Museum/University of Washington Press, 1998)

Bonnell, Victoria E., *Iconography of Power: Soviet Political Posters under Lenin and Stalin* (Berkeley: University of California Press, 1997)

Chelkowski, Peter and Hamid Dabashi, *Staging a Revolution: The Art of Persuasion in the Islamic Republic of Iran* (London: Booth-Clibborn Editions, 1999)

Cushing, Lincoln, *¡Revolución! Cuban Poster Art* (San Francisco: Chronicle Books, 2003)

Dickerman, Leah (ed.), *Building the Collective: Soviet Graphic Design 1917–1937* (New York: Princeton Architectural Press, 1996)

Evans, Harriet and Stephanie Donald (eds), *Picturing Power in the People's Republic of China: Posters of the Cultural Revolution* (Lanham, MD: Rowman & Littlefield Publishers, 1999)

Falasca-Zamponi, Simonetta, *Fascist Spectacle: The Aesthetics of Power in Mussolini's Italy* (Berkeley: University of California Press, 2000)

Frick, Richard (ed.), *The Tricontinental Solidarity Poster* (Bern: Comedia-Verlag, 2003)

Heller, Steven, 'Designing demons: the rhetoric of hate provides a different kind of meaning', *Eye* 41 (Autumn 2001), pp. 42–51

Heller, Steven, 'Designing heroes', *Eye* 43 (Spring 2002), pp. 46–55

Keen, Sam, *Faces of the Enemy: Reflections of the Hostile Imagination*, 2nd edn. (San Francisco: Harper and Row, 1988)

Kenez, Peter, *The Birth of the Propaganda State: Soviet Methods of Mass Mobilization, 1917–1929* (Cambridge: Cambridge University Press, 1985)

McQuiston, Liz, *Graphic Agitation: Social and Political Graphics Since the Sixties* (London: Phaidon, 2004)

Margolin, Victor, *The Struggle for Utopia: Rodchenko, Lissitzky, Moholy-Nagy, 1917–1946* (Chicago: University of Chicago Press, 1997)

Martin, Susan (ed.), *Decade of Protest: Political Posters from the United States, Vietnam, Cuba 1965–1975* (California: Smart Art Press, 1996)

Powell, Patricia and Shitao Huo, *Mao's Graphic Voice: Pictorial Posters from the Cultural Revolution* (Wisconsin: Elvehjem Art Center, 1996)

Poynor, Rick, 'A symbol returns to its true colours', *Eye* 40 (Summer 2001), pp. 8–9

Rhodes, Anthony, *Propaganda: The Art of Persuasion, World War II* (Chelsea House Publishers, 1976)

Sarhandi, Daoud and Alina Boboc, *Evil Doesn't Live Here: Posters from the Bosnian War* (London: Laurence King, 2001)

Schnapp, Jeffrey T., *Revolutionary Tides: The Art of the Political Poster 1914–1989* (Milan: Skira, 2005)

Timmers, Margaret (ed.), *The Power of the Poster* (London: V&A Publications, 1998)

Weill, Alain (ed.), *Affiches politiques et sociales* (Paris: Somogy, 1995)

Welch, David, *The Third Reich: Politics and Propaganda* (London: Routledge, 1993)

Wlassikof, Michel and Philippe Delangle, *Signes de la collaboration et de la Résistance* (Paris: Autrement, 2002)

Visual culture in the Arab world

AbiFares, Huda Smitshuijzen, *Arabic Typography: A Comprehensive Sourcebook* (London: Saqi Books, 2001)

Al-Fan al-Iraqi al-Mu'asser (*Contemporary Iraqi Art*), volume 1 – visual arts (Lausanne: Sartek, 1977)

Ali, Wijdan, *Modern Islamic Art: Development and Continuity* (Gainesville: University Press of Florida, 1997)

Arab Illustrators of Children's Books, catalogue of exhibition organized and presented by the Institut du Monde Arabe (13 June–31 August 2003) (Paris: Institut du Monde Arabe, 2003)

Atassi, Mouna and Samir Sayegh (eds), *Contemporary Art in Syria (1898–1998)* (Damascus: Gallery Atassi, 1998)

Azzawi, Dia' al-, *The Art of Posters in Iraq, a study of its beginning and development 1938–1973* (Iraq: Ministry of Culture and Information, Dar el-Rashid, Art Series, 1974)

Bahnisi, Afif, *Al-Fan wal-Qawmiya* (*Art and Nationalism*) (Damascus: Ministry of Culture and National Guidance, 1965)

Bahnisi, Afif, *Ruwad al-Fan al-Hadith fi al-Bilad al-Arabia* (*Pioneers of Modern Art in Arab Countries*) (Beirut: Dar al-Raed al-Arabi, 1985)

Bahnisi, Afif, *Al-Fan al-arabi al-hadith bayna al-hawiya wal-taba'iya* (*Arab Modern Art: Between Identity and Subjugation*) (Damascus: Dar al-Kitab al-Arabi, 1997)

Bartelt, Dana, 'Palestinian artists tell their people's story through symbols and allegory', *Eye* 51 (Spring 2004), pp. 54–9

Chakhtoura, Maria, *La guerre des graffiti, Liban 1975–1978* (Beirut: Dar An-Nahar, 1978)

Douglas, Allen and Fedwa Malti-Douglas, *Arab Comic Strips: Politics of an Emerging Mass Culture* (Bloomington: Indiana University Press, 1994)

Ettinghausen, Richard, *Arab Painting* (Geneva: Skira, 1977)

Fani, Michel, *Dictionnaire de la peinture au Liban* (Paris: Editions de l'Escalier, 1998)

Grabar, Oleg, *The Dome of the Rock* (Cambridge, MA: Harvard University Press, 2006)

Grabar, Oleg, *Islamic Visual Culture, 1100–1800* (Aldershot: Ashgate/Variorum, 2006)

Karnouk, Liliane, *Modern Egyptian Art, 1910–2003*, rev. edn. (Cairo: American University in Cairo Press, 2005)

L'affiche Palestinienne: Collection Ezzedine Kalak (Paris: Le Sycamore, 1979)

Lahoud, Edouard, *L'art contemporain au Liban* (Beyrouth: Dar el-Machreq Editeurs, 1974)

Massignon, Louis, *Les methodes de réalisation artistique des peuples de l'Islam* (Paris: P. Geuthner, 1921)

Mikdadi Nashashibi, Salwa (ed.), *Forces of Change: Artists of the Arab World* (Lafayette, CA: International Council for Women in the Arts, 1994)

Mikdashi, Hasna Reda and Nabil Ali-Shaath (eds), *Falastin fi Tawabe' al-Barid 1865–1981 (Palestine in postage stamps 1865–1981)*, 2nd edn. (Beirut: Dar al-Fata al-Arabi, 1985)

Naef, Silvia, *A la recherche d'une modernité arabe: l'évolution des arts plastiques en Egypte, au Liban et en Iraq* (Geneva: Slatkine, 1996)

Papadopoulo, Alexandre, *Islam and Muslim Art*, trans. Robert Erich Wolf (London: Thames & Hudson, 1980)

Rabi'i, Shawkat al-, *al-Fan al-Tashkili fi al-Fikr al-Arabi al-Thawri (Art in Arab Revolutionary Thought)* (Iraq: Ministry of Culture and Information, Dar el-Rashid, Art Series, 1979)

Safwat, Nabil, *The Art of the Pen: Calligraphy of the 14th to 20th Centuries* (London: Nour Foundation in association with Azimuth Editions and Oxford University Press, 1996)

Said, Shaker Hassan al- (ed.), *Hiwar al-Fan al-Tashkili (Visual Arts Dialogue: Conference on Aspects of Visual Culture and Its Relation to the Arab and Islamic Arts)* (Amman: Abd-el-Hamid Shuman-Darat alfounoun, 1995)

Scheid, Kirsten, 'The agency of art and the study of Arab modernity', *MIT Electronic Journal of Middle East Studies* 7 (Spring 2007)

Wedeen, Lisa, *Ambiguities of Domination: Politics, Rhetoric, and Symbols in Contemporary Syria* (Chicago: University of Chicago Press, 1999)

Lebanon history and politics

Abou, Selim, *Bechir Gemayel, ou, L'esprit d'un peuple* (Paris: Editions Anthropos, 1984)

Abou Khalil, Joseph, *Les Maronites dans la guerre du Liban* (Paris: Edifra, 1992)

Abu Khalil, As'ad, 'Druze, Sunni, and Shi'ite political leadership in present-day Lebanon', *Arab Studies Quarterly* vii/4 (Fall 1985), pp. 28–58

Ajami, Fouad, *The Vanished Imam* (Ithaca, NY: Cornell University Press, 1986)

Aulas, Marie-Christine, 'The socio-ideological development of the Maronite community: the emergence of the Phalanges and the Lebanese Forces', *Arab Studies Quarterly* vii/4 (Fall 1985), pp. 1–27

Beydoun, Ahmad, *Le Liban: itinéraires dans une guerre incivile* (Paris: Editions Karthala, 1993)

Binder, Leonard (ed.), *Politics in Lebanon* (New York: Wiley, 1996)

Chami, Joseph, *Chronicle of a War 1975–1990* (Beirut: Le Mémorial du Liban, 2005)

Corm, Georges, *Géopolitique du conflit Libanais* (Paris: La Découverte, 1986)

Dajani, Nabil, *Disoriented Media in a Fragmented Society: The Lebanese Experience* (Beirut: American University of Beirut, 1992)

Davis, Joyce M., *Martyrs: Innocence, Vengeance and Despair in the Middle East* (Hampshire: Palgrave Macmillan, 2003)

Fisk, Robert, *Pity the Nation: Lebanon at War* (Oxford: Oxford University Press, 1990)

Gellner, Ernest and John Waterbury (eds), *Patrons and Clients in Mediterranean Societies* (London: Duckworth, 1977)

Halawi, Majed, *Against the Current: The Political Mobilization of the Shi'a Community in Lebanon* (Ann Arbor, MI: UMI Dissertation Information Service, 1996)

Hamdan, Kamal, *Le conflit libanais: communautés religieuses, classes sociales et identité nationale* (France: Garnet, 1997)

Hanf, Theodore, *Coexistence in Wartime Lebanon: Decline of a State and Rise of a Nation* (London: Centre for Lebanese Studies in association with I.B.Tauris, 1993)

Harb, Mona, 'Know thy enemy: Hizbullah, "terrorism" and the politics of perception', *Third World Quarterly* xxvi/1 (2005), pp. 173–97

Harik, Judith, *The Public and Social Services of the Lebanese Militias* (Oxford: Centre for Lebanese Studies, 1994)

Johnson, Michael L., *Class and Client in Beirut: The Sunni Muslim Community and the Lebanese State, 1840–1985* (London: Ithaca Press, 1986)

Joumblatt, Kamal, *I Speak for Lebanon*, as recorded by Philippe Lapousterle, trans. Michael Pallis (London: Zed Press, 1982)

Kassir, Samir, *La guerre du Liban: de la dissension nationale au conflit régional: 1975–1982* (Paris: Editions Karthala, 1994)

Khalaf, Samir, *Lebanon's Predicament* (New York: Columbia University Press, 1987)

Khazen, Farid el-, 'Kamal Jumblatt, the uncrowned Druze prince of the left', *Middle Eastern Studies* xxiv/2 (April 1988), pp. 178–205

Khazen, Farid el-, *The Breakdown of the State in Lebanon, 1967–1976* (London: I.B.Tauris, 2000)

Khazen, Farid el-, 'Political parties in postwar Lebanon: parties in search of partisans', *Middle East Journal* lvii (Autumn 2003)

Khazen, Farid el-, 'Ending conflict in wartime Lebanon: reform, sovereignty and power, 1976–88', *Middle Eastern Studies* xl/1 (2004), pp. 65–84

Mohsen, Muhammad (ed.), *Al-Harb al-I'lamiya Namuzaj al-I'lam al-Muqawim fi Lubnan* (*The Media War: The Model of Media Resistance in Lebanon*) (Beirut: Dar al-Nada, 1998)

'Moslem and leftist organizations: Al Murabitoun', *Middle East Reporter*, 28 November 1987, pp. 7–9

'Moslem and leftist organizations: the Amal movement', *Middle East Reporter*, 31 October 1987, pp. 7–9

'Moslem and leftist organizations: Communist organizations', *Middle East Reporter*, 14 November 1987, pp. 9–10

'Moslem and leftist organizations: Hizbullah', *Middle East Reporter*, 7 November 1987, pp. 8–10

'Moslem and leftist organizations: the National Syrian Social Party', *Middle East Reporter*, 21 November 1987, pp. 7–9

Odeh, B.J., *Lebanon, Dynamics of Conflict: A Modern Political History* (London: Zed Books, 1985)

Pipes, Daniel, 'Radical politics and the Syrian Social Nationalist Party', *International Journal of Middle East Studies* xx/3 (August 1988), pp. 303–24

Qassem, Naim, *Hizbollah: The Story from Within*, trans. Dalia Khalil (London: Saqi, 2005)

Rabinovich, Itamar, *The War for Lebanon, 1970–1983* (Ithaca, NY: Cornell University Press, 1984)

Ranstorp, Magnus, *Hizb'allah in Lebanon: The Politics of the Western Hostage Crisis* (Hampshire: Macmillan, 1997)

Reuter, Christoph, *My Life Is a Weapon: A Modern History of Suicide Bombing* (Princeton, NJ: Princeton University Press, 2004)

Saadeh, Antun, *al-Muhadarat al'Asher 1948* (*The Ten Lectures 1948*) (Beirut: Syrian Social Nationalist Party, n.d.)

Saad-Ghorayeb, Amal, *Hizbu'llah: Politics and Religion* (London: Pluto Press, 2002)

Salibi, Kamal, 'The Lebanese identity', *Journal of Contemporary History* vi, 'Nationalism and Separatism' (1971), pp. 76–81, 83–6

Salibi, Kamal, *Crossroads to Civil War: Lebanon, 1958–76* (Delmar, NY: Caravan Books, 1976)

Seif, Roland, *Antoun Saadeh Za'im lil Mustaqbal* (Beirut: Meca, 1999)

Shams al-Din, Muhammad Mahdi, *Thawrat al Hussein: Zurufuha al-Ijtima'iya wa Atharaha al-Insaniya* (*The Revolution of al-Hussein: Its Social Circumstances and Human Effects*) (Beirut: Dar al-Ta'aruf lil-matbu'at, n.d.)

Shararah, Waddah, *Hurub al-Istitba'* (*Wars of Followership*) (Beirut: Dar at Tali'ah, 1979)

Shruru, Fadl, *Al-Ahzab wal-Tanzimat wal-Quwat al-Siyasiyya fi lubnan, 1930–1980* (*Political Parties, Organizations, and Forces in Lebanon, 1930–1980*) (Beirut: Dar al-Massira, 1981)

Snider, Lewis, 'The Lebanese Forces: their origins and role in Lebanon's politics', *Middle East Journal* xxxviii (Winter 1984), pp. 1–33

Snider, Lewis and Edward Haley (eds), *Lebanon in Crisis: Participants and Issues* (Syracuse, NY: Syracuse University Press, 1979)

Stoakes, Frank, 'The supervigilantes: the Lebanese Kataeb Party as a builder, surrogate and defender of the state', *Middle Eastern Studies* xi/3 (October 1975)

Tar Kovacs, Fadia Nassif, *Les rumeurs dans la guerre du Liban: les mots de la violence* (Paris: Editions du Centre National de la Recherche Scientifique, 1998)

Traboulsi, Fawwaz, *A History of Modern Lebanon* (London: Pluto Press, 2007)

Zubian, Sami, *Al-Haraka al-Wataniya al-Lubnaniya* (*The Lebanese National Movement*) (Beirut: Dar al-Massira, 1977)

POSTER CREDITS

Abdulfazl A'li (ed.), *The Graphic Art of the Islamic Revolution* (Tehran: Art Bureau of the Islamic Media Organization, 1985): figs 1.29–1.30

American University of Beirut, Library Special Collections and Archives, Beirut, Lebanon: figs 1.7, 1.17–1.18, 1.21, 1.26, 2.1–2.2, 2.4–2.5, 2.8, 2.12, 3.15, 3.18, 3.22–3.23, 4.18, 4.23–4.24, 4.38, 5.1, 5.3–5.4, 5.9, 5.11, 5.13–5.15, 5.17–5.19

Karl Bassil (poster collection), Beirut, Lebanon: figs 2.16, 3.4–3.5, 5.16

Abbudi Bou Jawde (poster collection), Beirut, Lebanon: figs 1.1, 3.1–3.3, 3.8–3.9, 3.16, 3.26, 4.1–4.4, 4.21, 4.29–4.34, 5.7

Hizbullah media office (poster archives), Beirut, Lebanon: figs 1.31, 2.19–2.22, 3.20, 3.27, 4.19, 4.25, 4.28, 4.35–4.37, 4.39–4.41, 5.5–5.6, 5.10, 5.25

Hoover Institution Archives Poster Collection, Stanford, California: figs 5.2, 5.21

Wassim Jabre (poster collection), Beirut, Lebanon: figs 3.12–3.13, 5.20, 5.22

Zeina Maasri (poster collection), Beirut, Lebanon: figs 1.2–1.6, 1.8–1.16, 1.19–1.20, 1.22–1.23, 1.27–1.28, 1.32, 2.3, 2.6–2.7, 2.9–2.11, 2.13, 2.15, 2.17–2.18, 3.6–3.7, 3.10–3.11, 3.14, 3.19, 3.21, 3.24, 3.28, 4.5–4.12, 4.15–4.17, 4.20, 4.22, 4.26–4.27, 5.8, 5.12

Progressive Socialist Party (poster archives), Mukhtara, Lebanon: figs 2.14, 3.17, 3.25

Photographic documentation of the Hizbullah poster archives by Agop Kanledjian

Poster scanning of the Karl Bassil, Abbudi Bou Jawde and Zeina Maasri collections by Future Graphics, Beirut

INDEX